Social Work Dept.

The
Behavior Disorder
IEP
Companion™

Objectives, Interventions, and Strategies

Molly Lyle Brown

Age Level:	5 thru 18
Grades:	K thru 12

LinguiSystems®

LinguiSystems, Inc.
3100 4th Avenue
East Moline, IL 61244-9700
1-800 PRO IDEA
1-800-776-4332

FAX: 1-800-577-4555
E-mail: service@linguisystems.com
Web: www.linguisystems.com
TDD: 1-800-933-8331
(for those with hearing impairments)

About the Author

L to R: Suzanne, Cathie, Molly, Jason

This book marks my first as a professional writer, though I have published "part-time" while teaching. No longer am I following the hectic schedules you are, trying to help students with little time or money to do so. The educational "alphabet" continues to call you, I know—IDEA, IEP, Content Standards, and NCLB. "What will it be next?" you ask. Something inevitably.

Hopefully this book will make your teaching life a tad easier and allow you time to actually enjoy your students. More importantly, I wish you the time and energy to enjoy your family, friends, and life in general more than ever before. World and personal events over the past three years have taught me much in how to live my life.

My 28 years in the education field has included teaching high school English and working as a resource teacher with students with special needs like learning disabilities, attention deficit hyperactivity disorder (ADHD), and autism. In addition to writing, I currently teach English Composition classes to students at the local community college, reaching a goal that I've had for a very long time. I have also worked as a writer and editor for LinguiSystems, Inc.

I have authored *100 Activities for Transition* with Hawthorne Educational Services, Inc., Columbia, MO, and *The LD Teacher's IEP Companion, The LD Teacher's IDEA Companion—K-5, The LD Teacher's IDEA Companion—6-12*, and *The ADHD Companion* with LinguiSystems, Inc. I am now writing *The LD Teacher's IEP Companion—Adolescents and Adults* to address their academic, transition, and post-secondary needs.

When I'm not teaching and writing, I spend time with my three wonderful daughters—Carrie, Kate, and Christie—and my four adorable grandchildren—Kayla, Sierra, Justin, and Jayden. I also enjoy running, lifting, biking, reading, socializing, and traveling.

Dedication

This book is dedicated to my students at Clinton High School, Clinton, Iowa. As I pursue other dreams and follow different paths in my education career, I will remember you. Thank you for teaching me how important it is to empower you, to let you learn "your" way, and to just let you "be."

This book is also dedicated to my "regular ed" colleagues who, side-by-side with me, taught all of our students in our "included" classes. To Cathie Adkins, Suzanne Rose, Josie McDermott, Kasey Lueders Jennings, Barb Brondyke, Jason McEwen, Wes Golden, and Angie Takes. You are all marvelous teachers!

Cover Design by Chris Claus
Page Layout by Jamie Bellagamba
Illustrations by Margaret Warner
Edited by Barb Truman

Table of Contents

Table of Contents, continued

Introduction

The Behavior Disorder IEP Companion is an easy-to-use professional resource with hundreds of IEP objectives as well as interventions or strategies for meeting those objectives. This resource will shorten the time it takes you to plan and write IEPs, leaving you valuable time for teaching and interacting with your students. It will also help you plan lessons and activities for your own classroom or in collaboration with regular educators who aid your students in developing appropriate behavioral skills.

The Behavior Disorder IEP Companion includes sections of objectives in areas where most students with behavior disorders have needs:

- improving academic performance
- meeting rules and expectations
- improving and developing interpersonal skills
- adapting behavior to school and classroom environment
- improving and developing self-management and self-esteem
- developing transition and employability skills

The objectives cover a broad range of academic, real-life, social, and behavioral skills appropriate for students as young as first grade to those students heading off to post-secondary institutions.

A section on diagnosing and assessing behavior disorders has been included to help you decide which students can benefit from programming in the area of behavior disorders. In addition, a section on handling behavioral issues in terms of your school discipline policy, and the needs and requirements stated through IDEA '97 is provided.

Most importantly, a section has been provided for you with general tips in instructing and setting up the classroom for students with behavior disorders, with particular emphasis on the current move toward positive behavioral supports. In some cases, extra tools like behavior monitoring charts and problem-solving sheets have been provided to facilitate your instruction.

What kinds of students benefit from *The Behavior Disorder IEP Companion*?

The Behavior Disorder IEP Companion is designed for use with students who exhibit behaviors that keep them from fitting into and succeeding in regular classrooms and in handling "normal," everyday social situations. Though designed for the student with behavior disorders, the objectives, strategies, and interventions are also appropriate in meeting the needs of many students served in special education and regular classrooms alike. These students may manifest behavioral and social difficulties due to a variety of disabilities like those listed on the next page.

- learning disabilities
- attention deficit disorder
- mild mental disabilities
- autism
- language or learning disabilities

Whether a student's behavioral difficulties are due to a skills or performance deficit, the objectives along with the strategies and interventions will help foster academic, social, and behavioral success. Students learn self-management strategies, problem-solving skills, and self-control techniques to help them get along with and gain acceptance from their peers and others.

Individual Objectives

Within each section of *The Behavior Disorder IEP Companion*, you'll find major goals listed for the year. The Individual Objectives suggested to meet each goal are worded so you can adapt them to fit one student or several students. They are also worded in such a way that you can implement the objectives within the regular classroom setting, in a resource room setting, or within the more restrictive environment of a classroom specifically for students with behavior disorders.

The Individual Objectives are either statements of the positive behaviors you want the student to exhibit instead of the inappropriate ones he displays now or statements of those behaviors that the student seems to lack and needs to learn.

The Individual Objectives suggested to meet each goal are worded so you can adapt them to fit the individual needs of your students. For example, one yearly goal is to meet the rules and expectations in the classroom. A sample IEP objective within this section states:

Objective: "The student will be able to act appropriately while seated."

For your purposes, you may need to add specific criteria and benchmarks related to how success is to be measured for an individual student. You may rewrite the objective and include benchmarks which say:

Objective: "Teron will be able to act appropriately while seated 75% of the time in math class."

Benchmark 1: can keep hands and legs to self
Benchmark 2: can raise hand to ask for teacher help
Benchmark 3: can whisper to another student when working together

Wording the objective and corresponding benchmarks this way may be appropriate for a student who is having significant difficulties sitting still and working independently.

Interventions or Strategies

For each IEP objective listed, *The Behavior Disorder IEP Companion* provides a strategy or an intervention that can be used in a variety of scenarios or situations. The strategy or intervention may be a description of prompts or reminders to encourage better behavior, an activity to teach a behavioral skill, or an approach to use to handle a given behavior in a particular circumstance. Many interventions or strategies may appear to overlap each other and you may see common threads in approaches, particularly as the student moves toward being able to manage his own behavior and improve his own behavior skills.

Recommended strategies or interventions have purposely been designed to accomplish the following:

- enhance motivation and self-control
- be usable in a variety of situations
- rely on inexpensive, easy-to-find materials
- be easily incorporated in daily academic lessons and other activities

You'll notice that some strategies or interventions suggest a form or chart for the student to use. Reproducible full-size copies of these forms and charts are provided in the Appendices for you to copy and use repeatedly with your students.

You'll find *The Behavior Disorder IEP Companion* valuable in not only creating individual education plans but also for facilitating collaborative planning and teaching among special and regular educators. I hope you find this book helpful in keeping the focus for students on positive behavior and effective learning.

Molly

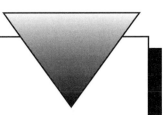

Teaching Students with Behavior Disorders

Some Guiding Thoughts and Principles

What, in theory and reality, can we actually do within the school setting, given seven or so hours a day with our students? After over 24 years in public school teaching, I'm pretty well grounded in reality. I've had my years of "trying to save the world" and every student who entered my classroom. I have learned that as much as I try, I can only set up the circumstances, do the appropriate teaching, keep parents and administrators informed, and then let things happen as they will.

I know that I can't control the student's family situation, address his medical needs, or do anything about past psychological factors. I can, however, control and do something about what's happening within the school setting. Luckily there are multiple strategies available today that help put the focus back on teaching rather than "disciplining and managing" such students. These teaching strategies help students learn, internalize, and become responsible for appropriate behavior.

Services for students with behavior disorders range from self-contained programs to multi-categorical resource programs. Some of our students with behavior disorders are served through 504 plans with primarily regular class placement. In my belief, many of our students with behavior disorders are very bright and can benefit from the positive role modeling provided by their peers in the regular classroom as long as there is adequate support provided to them. I have seen too many instances of students with behavior disorders "feeding off one another" when they're together too much, resulting in inappropriate behavior as the acceptable "norm" and part of their classroom culture.

I think the current trend toward "positive behavioral supports" (PBS) is a very good one in that it puts the focus where it should be—on helping students learn positive, acceptable behaviors. It takes planning, communication, and solid group effort, but the student with a behavior disability or disorder has his disorder in all scenarios all day long. A school- or building-wide focus provided by PBS can help make effective changes in systems that once created "holding tanks" for problem children, that meted out punitive consequences for inappropriate behavior and that, in the end, had little effect on improving actual student behavior.

What Are Positive Behavioral Supports (PBS)?

Through the 1997 reauthorization of IDEA (and depending on the reauthorization outcomes in 2003), IEP teams are required to use PBS to deal with behavior which is interfering with a student's learning and with the learning of others. The thought behind PBS is that actions and interventions, called "supports," can be used proactively with a student so that student is educated, rather than disciplined, as a means of improving behavior.

Four key concepts guide the choice of actions, interventions, and supports to use with a student. Positive Behavioral Supports must do the following:

1. Respond to the individual preferences, strengths, and needs of the student with the behavior problem.

2. Create changes in the environment when it is determined that the student's environment is helping to create the inappropriate behavior.

3. Teach new skills to the student with the inappropriate behavior so he learns appropriate responses.

4. Reinforce positive behaviors demonstrated by the student.

The intent of PBS is to tap all the constructive, educational resources available within a school system to help the student learn appropriate behavior, thus saving more extreme measures, like disciplinary action, as last resources.

The *Behavior Improvement Form* along with a completed example (pages 140-141) have been provided to lead you through the thinking needed in looking for and using positive behavioral supports within the school environment. The form may be used as a preliminary intervention to the more formal Behavior Intervention Plan (BIP) required if or when discipline issues arise.

Should actual disciplinary action become necessary, however, clear guidelines have also been set forth by IDEA '97 through a process called Functional Behavioral Assessment (FBA) as described in the next section.

Together, PBS as a proactive intervention and FBA as a reactive intervention look at systems, settings, and skill deficits as contributing to a student's problems rather than trying to fix the student himself. Positive behavioral supports teach students appropriate behavior rather than fixing bad behavior while also providing support for the physical and social contexts in which such behavior occurs.

The *Behavior Assessment Form* (page 142), *Behavior Tracking Sheet* (page 143), and *Student Behavior Survey* (page 145) are suggested as parts of the more formal FBA process initiated due to disciplinary action. (See flowchart page 13.). These forms may, in fact, be quite effectively used before that time in conjunction with PBS to provide a systematic approach to the student's behavior.

IDEA's Regulations for Serious Discipline Issues

According to IDEA '97, a functional behavioral assessment (FBA) must o[...]re or no later than 10 days after a disciplinary action, like a suspension. The FBA [...] that any behavioral intervention plan (BIP) developed for a student is purposely designed to meet a specific student's needs when serious behavioral and disciplinary infractions occur.

IDEA has also provided regulations for how school districts are to handle school suspensions that occur due to serious behavior by students with disabilities.

In the Case of Suspensions

If a student is facing suspension for disciplinary reasons, the following rules apply:

- Suspensions may be ordered for not more than 10 consecutive school days in the same school year, or suspensions may be ordered that total 10 school days in the school year.

    Schools do not need to provide services during the first 10 days in a school year that a student is removed. The school does not need to provide FAPE (free and appropriate public education) and the IEP team does not need to become involved.

- Handling of short-term removals after the initial 10 free (no service required) days is left up to the discretion of the school administrator in consultation with the student's special education teacher. They determine which services are to be provided during the short-term removal.

    A "change of placement" occurs if:

    the removal is for more than 10 consecutive school days, or the student faces a series of removals that appear to be a pattern and cumulate to more than 10 school days in a school year. Consideration of a pattern is based on factors such as the length of each removal, the total amount of time the student is removed, and the closeness of the removals to one another.

- Services are required on the 11th and subsequent days of a suspension. Such services are determined by the school administration and the student's special education teacher. The kinds of services must help the student progress in the general curriculum and achieve the goals set in his IEP.

    Regulations do not set a specific limit on the number of days students with disabilities can be removed from their current placement, as long as appropriate services are provided.

- Within 10 business days after the 11th day of suspension, the IEP team must plan and conduct a Functional Behavioral Assessment (FBA) and review an existing Behavior Intervention Plan (BIP). The IEP team must review how the BIP has been implemented and make any necessary changes to address the student's behavior.

When is a Functional Behavioral Assessment (FBA) required?

When it has been determined that a student has undergone a change in placement as described above or that the student has been removed from his current placement for more than 10 school days in a school year, the IEP team must conduct a Functional Behavioral Assessment. An FBA process might follow steps like those listed below.

1. First secure anecdotal information from teachers about the student's behavior in their classes. You'll want to find out if there's any pattern to where and when the student's behavior is occurring, or if the behavior occurs within one setting or in a certain type situation. Use the *Behavioral Assessment Form* on page 142 to facilitate collecting information from teachers or other staff members involved with the student.

2. Next collect some baseline data using the *Behavior Tracking Sheet* on page 143. Observe the behavior in a couple of different settings over a long enough period of time (e.g., two weeks) to get a realistic picture of the behavior. You may want a neutral observer that the student doesn't know to conduct the observations so that the student is unaware of the observation. A completed sample has also been provided for you on page 144. You might also want to use the *Behavior Tracking Sheet* to track when the student's behavior is appropriate so you have a basis of comparison. This will help you determine if and when the student has control over his behavior.

3. In addition, gather information from the student himself. One of the key components of the Manifestation Determination Process is concluding whether the student understands the impact and consequences of his behavior. With older students in particular, it makes sense to ask them what they understand. Use the *Student Behavior Survey* on page 145 to gather the results. (See the next page for a flowchart of the Manifestation Determination Process).

The Manifestation Determination Process

Any time a student is removed from school for more than 10 consecutive days or undergoes a change in placement, a Manifestation Determination must also be conducted in conjunction with a Functional Behavioral Assessment (FBA). The following flowchart describes a combined FBA and Manifestation Determination Process.

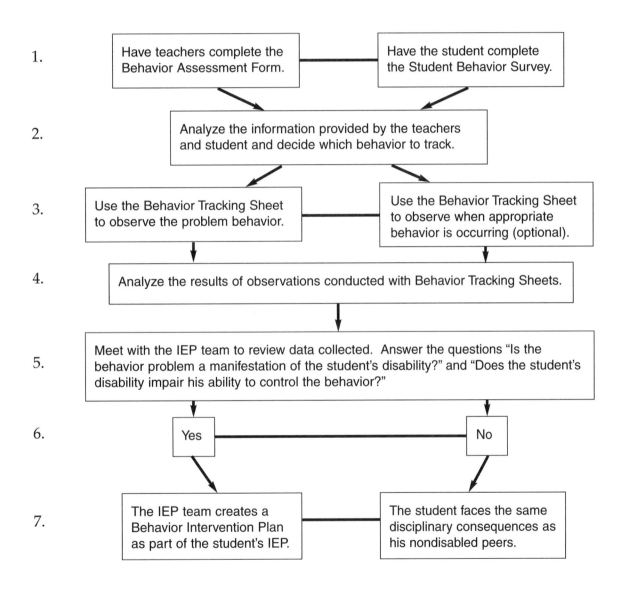

1. Have teachers complete the Behavior Assessment Form. | Have the student complete the Student Behavior Survey.

2. Analyze the information provided by the teachers and student and decide which behavior to track.

3. Use the Behavior Tracking Sheet to observe the problem behavior. | Use the Behavior Tracking Sheet to observe when appropriate behavior is occurring (optional).

4. Analyze the results of observations conducted with Behavior Tracking Sheets.

5. Meet with the IEP team to review data collected. Answer the questions "Is the behavior problem a manifestation of the student's disability?" and "Does the student's disability impair his ability to control the behavior?"

6. Yes | No

7. The IEP team creates a Behavior Intervention Plan as part of the student's IEP. | The student faces the same disciplinary consequences as his nondisabled peers.

Practical Tips for Program Success

Your behavior and attitude as a teacher along with the classroom environment you create are very important. They ensure the success of the programming and education you provide for your students with behavior disorders. Practical tips related to effective teaching behaviors and practices, classroom environments, and classroom organization are listed below.

Have patience. It goes without saying that any student will behave in such a manner as to "test the limits," especially the student with a behavior disorder. Ask yourself why the student is acting as she is or what she hopes to gain from her behavior rather than becoming exasperated or upset by it.

Keep your sense of humor. Some difficult situations can be defused with humor. If so, use it! Why get into power struggles when humor can "de-stress" a situation and possibly allow you and the student to talk about it?

Be firm and consistent. Students with behavior disorders need security and predictability even if they don't like your rules or expectations.

Give praise, praise, praise. Use praise and reinforcement for appropriate behavior. Ignore inappropriate behavior, if possible. After all, what you want is for your students to know how to behave well in given circumstances, and praising them lets them know they have learned and demonstrated appropriate behavior.

Be concrete. Use concrete, visual examples when you're explaining your behavioral expectations to students. Let students know exactly what you want so they don't become frustrated from guessing and missing the mark.

Take advantage of "teaching moments." Provide for the indirect, incidental and direct teaching of pro-social skills whenever the opportunity arises. If a student is exhibiting negative behavior, redirect the behavior and use it as a teaching opportunity for learning appropriate behavior.

Continually build students' self-esteem. By providing effective, direct instruction of appropriate behavior skills and encouraging the student's own intrinsic motivation (e.g., pride and social acceptance) to behave, the student's positive self-esteem will likely increase.

Please, no punishment! Avoid using punitive discipline measures unless they're needed as an absolute last resort. Punishment tends to demean students and lower self-confidence.

Let students problem solve. Teach your students conflict resolution and problem-solving skills so they can learn to appropriately handle situations independently.

Make learning good behavior part of your everyday curriculum. Provide for the proactive teaching of social, emotional and behavior skills as part of your and other teachers' everyday instruction. Students need direct, systematic instruction to learn appropriate skills and to carry them over to all situations in their daily lives.

Allow for practice. Give students frequent opportunities to practice social and behavior skills in environments where they can get praise, feedback, and redirection.

Help students develop self-control. Access and use self-inventories and monitoring forms that lead students toward self-monitoring and self-control.

Use proactive "time in" versus "time out" concepts. Keep the students within close proximity for a given period of time so they can be helped to behave appropriately.

Empower your students. Teach your students self-determination and self-advocacy strategies so they can get their own needs met effectively and appropriately.

Use peer models. Put your students with behavior disorders in as much contact with socially appropriate peers as possible so they can see and learn from good models of behavior.

Challenge your students. Keep students within the regular class setting as much as possible to both challenge their intellect and skills and to provide positive behavioral role models.

Be proactive. Anticipate your students' needs in situations so the needs can be addressed before "bad" behavior can occur. Students may need academic accommodations, environmental accommodations, or behavioral/social accommodations to be able to handle a task, situation, or activity.

Communicate! Let other teachers and school staff know about any accommodations and modifications a student might need to learn and behave well in their classroom. Be sure to communicate early on with your students' other teachers about their needs.

Creating an Effective Classroom Climate

Physical Arrangement

When you are arranging physical classroom space to adapt to your students' changing academic and social needs and individual needs, many things need to be considered. Taking time to thoroughly plan and think helps to enhance and provide opportunities for students to act appropriately and to avoid possible problems.

You can purposely organize the space in your classroom to positively affect students' behavior and attention by doing the following:

- Be aware of the location of each student.
- Keep track of the traffic flow within your classroom.
- Maintain a clear view of problem students.
- Closely observe and monitor peer relationships.
- Make accommodations for students' individual needs.

Rules and Expectations

In addition to monitoring your students' environment, it's also important to have rules and expectations so things go smoothly in the classroom. Doing the following will help:

- Efficiently manage your instructional time, particularly transitions between lessons and activities. Decide what students need to know and do to successfully complete one activity or lesson and make transitions to others.

- Create rules that all students will follow. Keep the rules at a minimum but reinforce them consistently. Consistent following of rules helps students develop cause-effect thinking for any rules or discipline to be effective.

- Determine the kinds of positive recognition students will receive for complying with the rules. Positive recognition can include praise, rewards, privileges, or other extrinsic motivators. Provide an area in your classroom for things like examples of good work, good behavior charts, lists of privileges students have earned, and so on.

- Create consequences for not following rules, ranging from first time occurrences to major infractions. Discuss and "publish" the consequences so students remain aware of them.

- Establish with your administration the policy for removing any student who exhibits violent or extremely disruptive, uncontrollable behavior. Decide what role any paraprofessionals or behavioral interventionists have in this process.

- Keep your students' parents informed about their students' behavior and academic success, both positive and negative. Parents can be very helpful in supporting you and reinforcing what the students are learning at school.

- Decide early on how to involve your consultant, psychologist, and administrators. You will need their support throughout the year so become familiar with their services and how they can help your students.

Improving Academic Skills

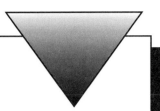

A sneer creeps across Nicole's face when she's asked if she has her assignment ready. Her body language radiates a loud "back off" message, so the teacher moves on past her, unwilling to engage in more confrontation. Three weeks ago, Nicole grudgingly took notes and attempted new math problems. Sure she grumbled once in a while, but that's part of Nicole's gruff exterior. Increasingly as the math concepts and processes have become more challenging, however, Nicole's academic attempts and her more cooperative attitude have waned and her surliness has resurfaced more often throughout the day.

Why isn't Nicole doing well academically? Are her behavior problems increasingly getting in the way of her academic success or are her academic difficulties causing her behavioral problems?

Many behaviors can have their roots in academic difficulties. The work the student is asked to do may be too difficult or it may not be meaningful to the student. Some students with behavior disorders may have learning disabilities or may deal with the effects of attention deficit disorder. Whatever the cause, some behavior problems may appear because of difficulties in the areas of regulating focus and attention, memory, language comprehension, inconsistent effort or motivation, organizational problems, or general academic skill weaknesses.

The objectives, strategies, and interventions in this chapter are designed to help your students improve academically by developing their skills in the following areas:

- paying attention
- staying on task
- completing tasks and activities
- following directions
- producing quality work
- working independently
- answering and asking questions
- participating in classroom discussion
- handling group activities
- performing in front of a group

 **Yearly Goal:** to develop and improve academic skills

Individual Objective	Strategy or Intervention
▶ Paying Attention	
1. The student will listen to verbal directions given by adults.	Most teachers have a "style" they've developed for direction giving as well as specific kinds of directions they've found most effective. Give students plenty of practice listening for verbal directions by teaching a specific unit or smaller units on verbal direction following. First think of all the kinds of verbal directions you might give. For example, you might give directions about how to write certain things on paper, how to cut or fold for projects, or how to move about the room for given activities. Choose directions you'll provide on a consistent basis for students to practice. After successful direction-following practice, reward students for their good listening and observation skills.
2. The student will sit and listen to stories.	Provide small stuffed animals or dolls/play action figures for younger students to hold onto as they listen. They may keep the animals or play figures during story time as long as they're listening attentively.

Older students may want to draw or doodle while they listen to help focus attention. Allow them to have a few colored pencils and paper at their desks as long as they're listening and quiet. Encourage them to draw about the events in the stories. |

Individual Objective	Strategy or Intervention
3. The student will quietly watch audio-visual presentations.	Give students a purpose for listening and/or watching. Create study guides for students to fill in as they watch. Or design a follow-up assignment to the audio-visual presentation that checks for understanding or prepares students for a follow-up discussion. Students are more focused and attentive when they know they will be held accountable.
4. The student will listen attentively to class speakers.	Prepare students ahead of time for outside class speakers. Tell them a little bit about the speaker's background as well as the topic she will address. When you arrange for the speaker to come, ask her to stop from time to time to allow students to ask questions. If possible, have the speaker provide you with a written topic outline ahead of time. Then have students think of questions related to the topic outline that they might ask when the speaker breaks for questions.
5. The student will listen attentively to peer presentations.	Most students enjoy when their peers make individual or group presentations. Use these presentations as incentives for students. Allow them to attend only if they have met prearranged guidelines. For example, a student might be expected to complete a given amount of homework for the week in that particular class prior to attending. Or the student may be expected to be attentive to classroom discussions and teacher presentations all week to show he has good listening and attending skills.

Individual Objective	Strategy or Intervention

▶ Staying On Task

1. The student will sit properly in his desk or space.

Seating Rules

All four chair legs on the floor.

Face forward.

Keep your legs under your desk.

Establish a couple of basic rules for sitting and consistently enforce them. Rules should cover safety and respect for property and space.

2. The student will work quietly at his seat.

Have available a variety of seating situations and options when students are expected to work quietly. For example, some students work better sitting alone in a beanbag chair or lying on the floor away from other students. Another student might need a study carrel so he can fidget and tap while he concentrates on work or listens to music with headphones. Allow flexibility in work arrangements as long as students work quietly and are productive.

3. The student will ignore distraction.

Try to eliminate as much visual or auditory distraction as possible. For example, during quiet independent work time, have any student needing help raise his hand and come to your desk. This way students around him won't be distracted by your discussion. Save things like passing papers back until the end of the period so quiet work times are not disrupted visually or auditorily.

Individual Objective	Strategy or Intervention

▶ Completing Tasks and Activities

1. The student will attempt new assignments willingly.

Preview the assignment and circle or highlight in color the sections you think the student can do more easily than others. Encourage the student to do those items first before requesting help or expressing frustration. Be available to give immediate feedback to the student when he completes the items. If necessary, build in effort grades as part of your grading system to encourage students who hesitate to try new things independently.

2. The student will persist with a task until it is completed.

Develop a check off system that can be used regularly for monitoring a student's work or activity while completing a task. For example, check the student's progress every five minutes during an at-seat assignment. If work is moving more toward completion, put a check in Check 1 and so on until the task or assignment is completed. Convert the check tallies to points for grading or an incentive as part of a reward system.

Work Completion Sheet

Student _____ Date _____

Class _____ Assignment or Task _____

    ❑ Check 1

    ❑ Check 2

    ❑ Check 3

    ❑ Check 4

    ❑ Completed

(reproducible full-size copy on page 146)

3. The student will complete class assignments during class time.

When you assign work, be sure the amount and difficulty level are suitable to the student's needs so he won't feel overwhelmed. Shorten the amount of work, if necessary, or break the assignment into two parts. The student can complete the first part and reward himself with a short break. Then the student can resume work with the next part. Part of the student's grade can be based on the amount of work done as well as its quality and accuracy.

Individual Objective	Strategy or Intervention
4. The student will complete tasks and assignments independently.	When a student is ready, have him carry an assignment book or assignment sheet. He should record assignments in the appropriate class spot and have the teacher sign off when the work is completed. If an assignment is homework, first the parent and then the teacher can sign off that work is complete. Allow the student to earn privileges or incentives weekly for completing work successfully and maintaining the assignment notebook.

Assignment Sheet

Class	Assignment	Teacher Initials	Parent Initials

(reproducible full-size copy on page 147)

5. The student will meet time lines for long-term assignments.

Provide students with a calendar or schedule of interim time lines they should meet in order to meet a final project or assignment time line. Build in points students can earn as part of their project grades if they meet these time lines as a way to discourage procrastination and encourage long-term planning and problem solving. Be sure to record points or check marks in your grade book as students meet their time lines.

Assignment: Illustrated Book of Plants

Time Line 1	October 25	Planning Stage: Outline and page layout of book.
Time Line 2	October 29	5 pages written or typed. Illustrations included.
Time Line 3	October 31	Total 10 pages written or typed. Illustrations included.
Time Line 4	November 1	Peer review of book. Make changes/corrections.
Final Due Date	November 4	Completed book due.

Individual Objective	Strategy or Intervention
6. The student will complete assigned homework.	Rather than having students record assignments in an assignment notebook, have them record individual class assignments on colored index cards or small colored sheets of paper. Colors can correspond to each class if you choose. The cards or paper should be small enough to fit inconspicuously in a pocket or tucked inside a textbook. As an incentive, the student can return the index card(s) the next day with a parent signature confirming assignment completion. A certain number of cards or completed assignments can be exchanged for extra grade points, rewards, or privileges.
7. The student will submit completed tasks and assignments.	It is important to have a consistent procedure and place for students to turn in completed assignments. First of all, write on the chalkboard in the same place every day what assignment is due as a reminder to students. Beside the assignment you've written, you can write messages like "We'll check in class and then hand in" or "Put your homework in the tray." Have a labeled tray or location in the room for students to hand in assignments that you'll be checking.

Within objective 6, a card illustration appears:

```
Name _____
Class _____
Assignment _____
        _____
Parent Signature _____
Date _____
```

Individual Objective	Strategy or Intervention
8. The student will remain on task during work time.	Estimate how long the assignment will take for the student to complete. Then tell the student what to do for the first half of the work time. Sticky notes are great for students to stick on their desks as reminders. Also write the time down when you expect the student to be done. When the student is finished, allow him to give the assignment to you for immediate praise, feedback, and grading. Then give the student the next part of the assignment to complete by the end of the work period.

Serena

Do questions 1, 2, 4, and 6. When you're done, take them to Ms. Brown for feedback.

Work is to be done by

Serena

Do questions 8, 9, 10, and the chart. Put your work in your Science folder when done.

9. The student will complete class work at his academic level.

A variety of skill levels and interests will exist among students with behavior disorders. Be prepared to offer a variety of learning options during instruction. One way to do so is to have a core lesson and activity for main concepts and then provide a variety of activities for students to choose from to complete other concepts you want to cover.

Lesson Activities Sheet

Lesson: Understanding Weather

Whole class: Notes and discussion on Weather and Meteorology
                            Read assigned textbook pages and answer assigned
                            questions.

Individual Choices: Choose one of these follow-up activities.

1. Prepare a TV weather map. Watch a forecast on TV for your area. Then make a map using colors and symbols to show the forecast for the next day.

2. Research Galileo's or another scientist's contribution to weather and meteorology. Create a written report and a visual aid to share with the class to illustrate this contribution.

3. Imagine you're a teacher responsible for helping four- and five-year-olds understand weather. Design a lesson to teach them about weather. Include material about types of weather and how it affects their everyday lives. How you teach the lesson and what activities you have them do is up to you.

4. Make a 3D weather project like a mobile, a map, or a model of a weather instrument.

5. Write the script for a weather report. Then audiotape or videotape your report.

(reproducible full-size copy on page 148)

Individual Objective	Strategy or Intervention

▶ Following Directions

1. The student will follow written directions for assignments.

Story Mapping Worksheet

1. Write the story title on the line.
2. Write what you think the story will be about on the line.
3. Read half the story. (Read to page 52.)
4. Fill in the story map with the name and description of important characters you know so far.
5. Finish reading the story.
6. Fill in the most important events that happened, including the story's ending.
7. Add any other characters and descriptions to the story map.

Story Title _____

I think the story will be about _____.

Character Name

Character Description

Character Name

Character Description

Character Name

Character Description

Event

Event

(reproducible full-size copy on page 149)

Make sure that written directions are presented in as short and concise language as possible. If students need to follow the directions one step at a time, present the directions as a list of steps. Students can then move to or check off each step of directions as it is completed. Boxing or otherwise isolating directions and creating white space for easy reading on the worksheet can also help direction following.

2. The student will follow verbal directions for assignments.

First of all, cue students visually and/or verbally that you are about to present verbal directions. You might raise your arm and say, "Look at me. I'm about to give you directions for the next activity." Wait for students to be attentive. Be consistent with the cue(s) you use each time so students make it a habit to listen upon cueing. Then proceed to give the verbal directions. Be sure to pause a few seconds after each step of the direction to assess that listening and understanding are occurring. You can usually tell by the looks on students' faces and if anyone is raising a hand. Ask students to put questions off until you're done so you can keep attention focused. Try not to get in the habit of repeating directions as that encourages students to take less responsibility for their own attentiveness.

Individual Objective	Strategy or Intervention
3. The student will follow test directions.	First analyze the best way to test a student to accurately show his skills and knowledge. For example, one student might respond well to broad open-ended essay questions that allow him to show how he has synthesized and applied what he's learned. Another student might respond better to fill-in questions with a word bank or to multiple choice. Then test the student in the same way each time with the same set of directions.

▶ **Producing Quality Work**

Individual Objective	Strategy or Intervention
1. The student will turn in neat papers.	Be sure to be very specific about what neat means to you. Does it mean no erasures, all work completed in ink, answers written in legible cursive, or no paper torn from a notebook? Students need to know the criteria for neatness for each teacher they have in order to meet expectations for neat work.

Some students may need to hand papers in immediately to keep them clean, unrumpled, legible, and otherwise neat. Provide an individual file folder for students whose papers aren't always neat. Depending on students' levels of organization and responsibility, they can either keep the folders in trappers or notebooks, or you can provide a spot in the room for students to consistently place folders with completed assignments. |

Individual Objective	Strategy or Intervention
2. The student will be able to check his own work for errors.	Students need to learn "teacher skills" to be able to check their own work for errors. After the student completes his assignment, have him signal to you that he is done. Then, while sitting beside the student, have him talk through each question or problem with you, checking for correctness. Coach the student on what criteria to look for in correcting that particular assignment. Hopefully, after a few "coaching" sessions, the student can review assignments on his own.
3. The student will be able to accept corrections of school work.	Allow the student to improve his performance on selected papers. For example, in science or math class, it may be important to master certain concepts before moving on to the next skill or concept. Let the student correct his work and gain a percentage of "improvement points" or move up an assignment grade. Be clear about when corrected work is due, preferably within the next day or two, so it has a positive impact on furthering his skills or knowledge.
4. The student will be able to make use of corrections of school work.	Make answer keys available to students to check their own work. Make sure they check their assignments using a different colored marker or pen so they aren't tempted to "fix" their answers. To encourage learning from errors, allow the students to redo some missed questions or have a short practice reinforcement sheet to do and then add that score to the original grade. However, if the students are more accurate the first time because of close checking (not needing to redo), their final grade will be higher.

Individual Objective	Strategy or Intervention
5. The student will be able to produce work of good quality and accuracy.	For every assignment or project you assign the student, make a printed list of the criteria you expect to be followed to produce a quality assignment or project. Put the list on the board as well as give the student an individual copy. Keep the list to a minimum of three or four descriptors so quality is attainable for the student. Descriptors might include things like the following. Include specific information like page length or number of problems as needed.

For math:
show steps and work done to arrive at a solution
neatness/legibility
accuracy of answers

For a written assignment:
meets length requirement
meets goal of assignment (e.g., description, narration, persuasion)

For a project:
must be 3-dimensional
shows creativity/originality
meets due date

For longer-term or more complex papers or projects, be sure to have concrete models and examples for the student to look at. Make the models and examples available for reference until the student is done. |

▶ Working Independently

1. The student will be able to handle free time.	Provide limited, consistent options for the student during any free time. For a younger student, computer time, reading corner time, or quiet play may be provided as options for the student to choose from. Older students might use computer time, listening with headphones to a CD in a separate spot, or reading a magazine quietly during any free time.

Individual Objective	**Strategy or Intervention**
2. The student will begin assignments independently.	Create an assignment folder for the student. If assignments are provided for multiple classes, clearly label which assignments are for which class. Then at the given work time, the student can get his assignment folder and begin work on his own. Create a reward or point system for the student who cooperates with this part of the daily routine. Completed assignments should be returned to the folder for grading and comments.
3. The student will arrange for individual accommodations as needed.	Students often need accommodations on an individual assignment-by-assignment basis depending on skill expectations and difficulty level. Initially sit down with each student as he receives an assignment. Discuss what he'll need to do to complete the assignment by using a sheet like the one on the left. Talk about the skills and time required and decide if the assignment is within the student's capabilities. If not, together you and the student can arrange for necessary accommodations or alternatives. After a few "coaching sessions," encourage the student to review his own assignments and request accommodations. Make sure students understand that they need to request accommodations when they first receive the assignment, not days later when procrastination or something else has interfered with their abilities to complete it.

Request for Accommodations

Class: Social Studies

Assignment: Draw a map of the U.S. Then color and label each state.

Skills Needed: drawing, coloring, neat printing, spelling

Time Given: 1 day

Accommodations: Chris will need:

1. Extra time — 2 days to complete
2. A pre-drawn map of the U.S. with state borders included
3. Extra help with spelling of states' names

Date: May 9   **Teacher**: Mrs. Truman

(reproducible full-size copy on page 150)

4. The student will manage test anxiety.	Develop a study guide for the student to use prior to the test. Include the major concepts, skills, and processes that will be covered on the test. As part of the study guide, also include a practice test for the student to complete that is similar in length and format to the test he will actually take. Review and grade the student's study guide and test work prior to the student taking the test.

Individual Objective	Strategy or Intervention
5. The student will have materials available to complete assignments.	Many students will get to work willingly if materials are available to them and they don't get so frustrated looking for them that they can't work. Rather than fight the battle of disorganization, create a flexible and efficient supply system. At the beginning of a semester or school year, have students bring a given amount of materials, like paper, pencils, crayons, and rulers. Provide a spot in the room for students to store those materials, either as a class supply available to everyone or as individual supplies in small boxes. Textbooks and workbooks may also be kept in the classroom as well as creating a given spot for worksheets to be used that day.

At the beginning of the class, list the materials needed that day on the chalkboard in a consistent spot. Immediately when students enter the room, they are to get the materials needed, sit down, and be ready to work. |
| 6. The student will be able to take written notes when directed. | Cue students when they need to take notes by saying something like "You need to take out your notebooks and write down what we're going over today." Make sure to have typed copies of the notes available both as overhead transparencies and paper copies for student use. As you go over the notes, show students only what you're discussing and allow them ample time to copy. After they copy, review the portion of the notes so they aren't trying to focus on too many things at once. Students who use the paper copies should keep pace with your notes and discussion. |

Materials Needed Today:

pencil
ruler
two colored pencils
graph paper
Math workbook

Individual Objective	Strategy or Intervention
▶ **Answering/Asking Questions**	
1. The student will try to answer questions when called on.	When asking questions, build in appropriate wait time for the student to have time to think of an answer. If needed, break the question down into smaller sub questions to guide the student's thinking. Once the student attempts an answer, tell him "Thank you for your ideas" and move on to another student or ask another question of the class to expand the discussion further. Always thank and praise students who cooperate and try.
2. The student will be able to say he does not know an answer in an appropriate manner.	Role-play and rehearse with the student possible ways to turn down answering a question while also "saving face" with peers. The student might say simply "I'm not able to answer that question" or "Can you give me a shot at another question later on?" or another appropriate response you both agree on. As long as the student responds appropriately and respectfully, go on to another student.
3. The student will be able to volunteer answers to teacher's questions.	When students work independently, use that as an opportunity to get to know students individually. Frequently pull up a chair and have them walk through the thinking process they're using to complete their work. The student will become more comfortable with your questioning style and you will learn what kinds of questions the student is able to answer so class discussions will be more comfortable and productive.

Individual Objective	Strategy or Intervention
4. The student will be able to ask appropriate questions during discussions.	With the student, preview ahead of time what will be discussed during a particular class discussion. For example, the day before or if necessary when the student walks into class, briefly tell him what the discussion topic will be. Together, have him formulate one question that will be appropriate to ask. The "preview" lets more hesitant students prepare, while for other students it screens out possibly inappropriate or irrelevant questions or comments.

▶ Participating in Classroom Discussion

1. The student will be able to discuss contrary opinions during class discussions.	Lay the groundwork for civil discussion within your class when contrary opinions will be presented. Establish rules for respecting differences of opinion without having students come across as attacking others for their views. With the class, discuss the difference in using emotionally-laden words like *stupid* versus saying something is not well thought out or is narrow-minded. Give plenty of examples to illustrate the difference. If you have to, ban certain words from discussion like *stupid*, *sucks*, *lame*, and *gay* to encourage more neutral vocabulary.
2. The student will be able to use an appropriate tone of voice in class discussions.	Rehearse appropriate voice level with your students. Role-play a student speaking softly from the back. Also role-play a student talking over others. As you role-play, allow a small group of students to stand where you would be and also where other classmates might be. Discuss how in both instances, you and classmates can't hear the discussion. As a class, determine the appropriate voice level. Also talk about how you or other students might signal to a speaker that his voice tone needs to be more appropriate.

Individual Objective	Strategy or Intervention
3. The student will be able to participate in class discussions conducted by the teacher.	To encourage the student to participate, build discussion points into your grading system. Set a given goal for the student to reach to acquire his points. For example, a student might be expected to contribute two times during the week in reading class. If possible, let the student know the discussion topics ahead of time so he'll be prepared and more comfortable participating.
4. The student will be able to provide reasons for the opinions he expresses.	On a regular basis, have students support and explain their thinking. On essay tests, assigned worksheets, and in small group activities, frequently provide opportunities to practice supporting opinions using facts and concepts students learn in their academic subjects. Choose these opportunities for thinking and applying concepts rather than having students simply regurgitate memorized information.
5. The student will be able to share relevant items during class discussions.	Before class, on either the same day or possibly the day before, let the student know what the discussion topic will be. The student will then be able to think of relevant information and experiences related to the topic. If the student's comment is not relevant, praise and redirect him, saying, "James, I'm glad you're adding to the discussion. Keep your comments on the topic, okay?"

Improving Academic Skills
The Behavior Disorder IEP Companion

Individual Objective	Strategy or Intervention

▶ Handling Group Activities

1. The student will participate in group activities.

Group Planning Sheet

Assignment: Math Word Problems

Group: four members

Role of Group Member 1: Problem Setup

Responsibility: Read the word problem; set up the computation steps for solving.

Role of Group Member 2: Solve Problem

Responsibility: Also read the word problem; review computation steps for accuracy; solve the problem.

Role of Group Member 3: Check Work

Responsibility: Using a calculator, check Group Member 2's computation.

Role of Group Member 4: Write Answer

Responsibility: Write answer(s) legibly and neatly; put answers in appropriate spaces on answer sheet.

(reproducible full-size copy on page 151)

When a group is formed for an activity or for a game, make sure each group member has a given role. When members have given roles, they're more likely to actively participate than to be passive observers.

For example, a student might be the scorekeeper in a group playing a game or the answer checker in a group that's working to complete an assignment. Be sure to hand group members written descriptions of their roles so they have them to refer to.

2. The student will play cooperatively with other children or peers.

Whether on the playground or in the classroom, set up game playing situations on a regular basis. Keep group sizes small, perhaps no larger than three or four students. If possible, keep the same students together until they become a well-functioning and cooperative group. As needed, and with the student's permission, inform other group members of a particular member's difficulties and needs so they can be supportive and help the student play and interact cooperatively.

Individual Objective	Strategy or Intervention
3. The student will share materials appropriately.	Set concrete parameters for how many materials a student may borrow at a time. For example, if students are coloring a project, tell them they may have only two crayons or markers in their possession at one time and that when they are done using the materials, to return them to the appropriate container for others to use. If there is a specific way to take care of something before it is returned, demonstrate for students and then have them return it. For example, students may need to tighten and wipe off glue tops before returning the containers so the glue doesn't dry out.
4. The student will work cooperatively with another partner.	Sometimes working with a partner may be too stimulating or stressful for a student. To make the situation more comfortable, allow students to choose partners as long as they are compatible. Then allow partners to work in different areas where they're comfortable. For example, one set of partners may work better in a corner in the back of the room, in the library, or outside the door in the hallway.
5. The student will initiate and assist in conducting a group activity.	On a regular basis (e.g., weekly), allow a free-choice group activity. Rotate who chooses the activity so each group member has a chance to choose and lead. Have consistent group members so students become comfortable working with and leading one another. Group activities can include things like board games, computer games, and art projects.

Individual Objective	Strategy or Intervention

▶ **Performing in Front of a Group**

1. The student will participate in role playing.

Explain to your entire class that role playing will be a technique you'll use frequently to teach and practice certain skills in your classroom. Then let students choose role playing partners they'll have for an extended period of time. Allow the choices as long as students are productive and cooperative. Use role plays several times a week for practicing problem solving, applying newly acquired social skills, or reviewing academic concepts. If larger role-play groups are needed, put two sets of partners together.

2. The student will be able to read aloud to a small group.

Keep groups small with no more than two or three students. Select students who will be supportive of one another and not make fun when someone stumbles over a word. Maintain the reading groups for a long period of time so students become comfortable and confident reading for others.

3. The student will be able to read aloud for the entire class.

Let the more reluctant or weaker reader know what he'll be reading aloud ahead of time. For example, if you're reading a play, assign parts one day and have students review the characters' reading parts before reading them the next day. Or if the class is reading a short story, give the student a copy of the page he'll be reading from with the section highlighted for better focus and attention.

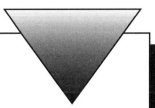

Meeting Rules and Expectations

Tyson makes a leap for the door (jamb), swinging his body over the "line" and technically "in" before the bell rings, consequently avoiding a tardy. This is his routine for the first couple days of class. Then the classroom rule expands to include "being in your seat" when the bell rings to be on time and ready for class. Of course, that rule doesn't encompass Tyson's chattering (and he isn't the only one) that continues even as the teacher attempts to get the students' attention. And throughout the class period, Tyson blurts out comments to Mike who sits across the room, thus interrupting the lesson flow for everyone.

Whew!!!!!! So much behavior to deal with, so many "loopholes of understanding" of the rules to anticipate—that's the challenge of regular and special education teachers alike who interact with students with behavior management difficulties every day.

Rules and expectations protect and respect the student, the environment, other students, and our mission of learning together. To provide this respect and protection, it is extremely important to have consistent rules, routines, and expectations for every student, and particularly for those with erratic behaviors and inconsistent needs. You can best create a healthy, supportive, consistent learning environment by doing the following:

- stating rules positively
- having consistent rules and routines
- providing the student with clear statements and descriptors of desired behavior
- describing the consequences of not behaving
- setting clear limits and boundaries for behavior
- helping students meet the overall expectations of the school in general

The objectives, strategies, and interventions in this chapter will help your students successfully meet the rules and expectations of your classroom and school.

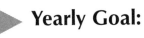 **Yearly Goal:** to improve the ability to respect and follow school and classroom rules and expectations

Individual Objective	Strategy or Intervention
1. The student will be able to follow a daily routine.	Provide written copies of the daily routine on a large poster at the front of the room and on individual copies students may keep at their desks. Daily routines or schedules may cover individual classes or chunks of the day depending on grade levels and needs of the students. When there is a change in routine or schedule, prepare students the day before as well as the day of the change so the transition goes smoothly. Students can copy the changed routine or schedule onto notebook paper to help them remember.
2. The student will seek permission before leaving her seat.	From the very first day in your classroom, establish legitimate reasons for getting out of one's seat and how to ask permission. For example, coach students to raise their hands, patiently wait to be recognized, and then ask, "May I leave my seat to _____?" A student with attentional difficulties may be restless and need to move to expend excess energy, allowing her to then get back on task. Have a predetermined area the student may move to. To ask permission, this student might say, "May I get up and move around for a minute?"

Individual Objective	**Strategy or Intervention**
3. The student will remain quiet and on task during work time. **Jayden's On-Task Tally Chart** You're "on task" when you are: ☐ sitting quietly at your seat ☐ working on the assignment ☐ appropriately raising your hand for help ☐ working quietly with a peer 	Date	Class	On-Task Tally Marks	Comments
---	---	---	---
September 8	Reading	///	Good working today! Ms. B		Prepare a small chart for the student on which you can make tally marks to record when she is on task. Be sure to describe what on-task behavior looks like for your purposes. During given time intervals (e.g., every five minutes), pass by the student's desk and check for on-task behavior. Give the student a tally mark if she is on task. Later you might convert tally marks to extra assignment points or to other pre-established rewards. At some point, to encourage internal control by the student, allow the student to check her own on-task behavior and make tally marks at given time intervals.
4. The student will come to class on time. **Class Sign-In Sheet** Class _____ Period _____ Teacher _____ 	Student's Name	Time In	Minutes Late/On Time	Reason
---	---	---	---
Dan Landon	8:58	3	overslept - missed first period class
Leatha Johnson	8:59	4	talking to friends
				  (reproducible full-size copy on page 152)	Create a sign-in book or sheet (like the one on the left) for individual students who exhibit chronic lateness. The sign-in sheet can serve several purposes: • assess how much time is being missed and determine why (and even why they did succeed in being on time) • allow for problem solving • create reward systems for the student who becomes more punctual • serve as documentation of problems needing referral to administration

Individual Objective	Strategy or Intervention
5. The student will follow rules on the playground, in the lunchroom, in the library, and in other designated areas.	Have the supervisors of each area review rules with students the first few times they go to the area. Encourage supervisors to state the rules in positive ways so the expectation is that students will exhibit good behavior. Display "rules" posters in very visible areas as reminders to students.

Lunchroom Rules

1. You may talk in conversational tones.
2. Stay in your seat throughout the lunch time.
3. Please put your trash in the bins and your trays on the carts.

Thank you for keeping our lunchroom a nice place!

---

6. The student will be able to act appropriately while seated.

Observation Sheet

Student _____Kurtis Carter_____
Observer _____Eric Gomez, Teacher_____

Date	Class	Behaviors Observed	Number of Times Observed
4/12	Math	Trouble keeping hands to himself during independent work time.	〼

(reproducible full-size copy on page 153)

The first thing to determine is what behaviors the student exhibits that are inappropriate as well as appropriate. There can be many reasons why a student is uncooperative or inattentive while seated. Make observations for several days to see if there is a pattern. If the student is in classes with other teachers, have those teachers make observations too. Compile the results of your observations and note any circumstantial or behavioral patterns. Use the results to develop more concrete rules and guidelines for the student, to make seat changes, or to make accommodations in assignments.

7. The student will be able to handle constructive feedback and redirection from the teacher.

Discuss privately with each individual student the best way to provide constructive feedback and redirection. One student may prefer to stay after class to review work, while another may prefer that comments and directions be written on a separate sheet of paper to refer to as she makes changes. Allow students to raise grades or earn extra points by making revisions and improvements to their work.

Individual Objective	Strategy or Intervention
8. The student will be able to follow school rules.	Many schools have written handbooks or handouts describing their attendance and disciplinary rules. For younger students or students with reading difficulties, you may need to modify the rules by adding pictures or simplifying the language so students can easily understand them. Early in the semester or school year, review the handbooks with students as actual instructional lessons during the school day (e.g., during your language arts or social studies classes). Be sure that students' parents also receive copies of handbooks or modified rules.
9. The student will not bring illegal or inappropriate materials to school.	Students with behavior disorders will need explicit, concrete descriptions of what the school considers illegal and inappropriate. Invite your police liaison officer or an officer from your community to speak to your students. Have the officer describe illegal and inappropriate materials to your students and the consequences for possessing them both at school and in the community. (Suggest to the officer to bring photos of illegal and inappropriate materials as examples so students understand better.) A few days later, have a school administrator follow up the officer's presentation to reinforce the rules and consequences.

Individual Objective	Strategy or Intervention
10. The student will understand the consequences of her own behavior.	With your students, develop a chart to show the consequences of particular behavior in your classroom and school in general. Be sure to set degrees of consequences as well as parameters for behavior as you make the chart. Make individual copies for students as needed, as well as copies to post in the room.

Behavior	Consequences
Talking/Off Task Chronic Talking/Off Task (3 warnings) Refusal to Follow Warning	Teacher Warning Parent Contact Office Referral
Swearing Chronic Swearing (3 warnings) Refusal to Follow Warning	Teacher Warning Parent Contact Office Referral
Incomplete Work Chronic Late Work (3 missing assignments) Refusal to Follow Warning	Reminder and Grade Deduction Parent Contact Removal of Privileges

Individual Objective	Strategy or Intervention
11. The student will dress for P.E. class.	If possible, discuss with the student why she is not dressing for P.E. If the student willingly participates in P.E. except for getting dressed, consider accommodations like the following:

• allow street clothes to be worn
• provide a more private place for dressing
• have school provide appropriate clothes for P.E.
• reward points or other incentives for dressing |

Individual Objective	Strategy or Intervention
12. The student will participate appropriately in P.E. class.	Set a minimum criteria for the student to "pass" or gain credit for P.E. For example, the student might be expected to walk 20 minutes around the track to pass for the day. Using a Pass/Fail grading system would be an appropriate accommodation under such circumstances.
13. The student will be able to follow the rules or guidelines for an activity.	Partner two students you think might work well together. Provide activity rules or guidelines verbally and in writing, giving each student a copy. Students can check off each guideline as it's followed. Let the students earn a shared grade for following guidelines and working cooperatively together.

Weather Mobile (2nd grade)

1. Cut out or draw pictures related to weather.
2. Glue the pictures on sturdy cardboard pieces to fit each picture.
3. Use a paper hole puncher to put holes in the pictures for hanging.
4. Tie string or yarn to each picture.
5. Tie each picture to the hanger.
6. Present the mobile together to the class.

Weather Forecast (7th grade)

1. Choose a country and one of its major cities to prepare a forecast for.
2. Using the Internet, research the current weather conditions. Include the temperature, humidity, barometric pressure, precipitation, and any other relevant environmental conditions (e.g., water shortage, forest fires, avalanches).
3. Write a script of what you'll say during the forecast.
4. Create visual aids for your presentation.
5. Rehearse the script using your visual aids.
6. Present your forecast to the class. You will be videotaped!

Individual Objective	Strategy or Intervention
14. The student will be able to take appropriate care of personal property.	To encourage proper care of personal property, ensure it happens as part of the student's daily routine. At the beginning of the school year, have students bring in school supplies and other items they need and label them with their names. Also, if books are checked out, assign numbers and names to them. Each day or each period, depending on grade level, have a "pack up and put away time." Storage can occur in a given place in the room or in a student's locker. If possible, reward students with points or incentives for good care, like intact pencils, organized notebooks, or neatly stored books.
15. The student will be able to raise her hand and wait her turn to speak.	Begin with small group discussions to practice having students raise their hands and wait turns. For example, while other students are working on independent seat work, one small group can hold a discussion related to the topic. If an assistant is available, have her conduct the discussion while you're assisting individual students in class or vice versa depending on the class. As students become more adept at turn taking, move on to having them participate in a larger group and then eventually with the whole class.

Individual Objective	Strategy or Intervention
16. The student will be able to appropriately signal for help from the teacher.	For younger students, role-play how you want them to ask for help. If you're somewhere far away from the student, the student can patiently raise her hand and remain quiet. Tell the student you may not instantly see her signal, but she is to remain seated with her hand up and sit quietly. If you are nearby, the student might say in a normal voice tone, "Ms. Medoza, would you help me please?" Role-play several days in a row when you and the students are first getting to know each other. For older students or students who may be more self-conscious about requesting help, tell them you'll scan the room frequently and walk around to see how everyone is doing. Students can signal for help by raising their writing utensils. In either case, be sure to respond only to students who follow given signals.
17. The student will be able to be patient and act appropriately while waiting for assistance.	In a busy classroom, it may be difficult to get to a particularly needy student quickly. If possible, arrange for another student who can be a patient role model to act as intermediary help. When you can, provide help directly to the student, praising her for appropriate behavior.
18. The student will be able to follow teacher and classroom rules. 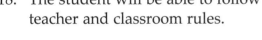Rules in Math Class 1. Quietly ask a buddy for help. 2. Show all your work. 3. Return borrowed calculators.	Prioritize the rules most important for a student to follow and state them concisely so she can remember and learn them. For example, for each of the student's teachers and classrooms, choose the three rules most important for the student to follow for success there. The student can keep the rules on a note card at her desk or on a page inside a notebook. Have the classroom teacher regularly praise the student for following a rule. For example, a teacher might say, "It really helps when you work quietly at your seat. Thank you, Sasha, for doing that."

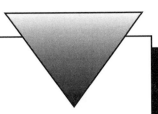

Adapting Behavior to School and Classroom Environment

For just a few moments, imagine taking a trip back in time to your very first day of school. What fears and trepidations do you suppose you had? Was the idea of the bus and all those people or the big school building somewhat frightening? What things might have excited you at that tender age? How long do you think it took before school felt "old hat" or routine and comfortable for you?

For many of our students, that "fitting in" to the school and classroom environment is a tremendous learning and behavioral challenge. These students have to learn how to manage on the school bus, crossing the street, entering the school building, as well as moving around from classroom to classroom, and leaving the building in supervised and unsupervised circumstances. Somehow for them, there is a hidden behavioral curriculum of acceptable behavior that they must acquire to meet overall success within the school and classroom environment.

Through our instruction and our management of the environment, we can provide these students with the consistency, comfort, and security they need to learn more appropriate behavior and ways of coping and handling the environmental expectations of school.

The objectives, strategies, and interventions in this chapter will help your students adapt and successfully fit into your school and classroom environment by learning how to do the following:

- care for the school and classroom environment
- handle emergencies at school
- cope in the lunchroom
- move around the school environment

Yearly Goal: to adapt to and respect the school and classroom environment

Individual Objective	Strategy or Intervention
▶ **Caring for the School and Classroom Environment**	
1. The student will put away toys and materials with supervision.	Supervise the student at his own level rather than standing over him and coercing cooperation. Either seated on the floor or on a nearby chair, help the student put things away by working together with him or by making a game of it. You might say something like, "I see something blue that belongs on the shelf."
2. The student will put away toys independently.	Initially enlist the help of another student to be a partner for the student you are working with. At a given consistent signal, like "It's time to put things away," the partner should offer to help the student put things away. Keep student partners together until the individual student indicates he's ready to put things away on his own.
3. The student will use classroom equipment and materials correctly.	Provide only a limited number of materials or equipment for students to use at any one time. This will make it easier for students to manage and easier for you to supervise. Demonstrate for students how to use the item and then how to care for it and put it away.

Individual Objective	Strategy or Intervention
4. The student will use playground equipment safely.	Organize students at stations for turn taking on particular pieces of equipment. For example, three students might be allowed on the slide at one time while another three are climbing the jungle gym. That way, you can oversee a student's safety on equipment as well as provide equal time on equipment for students.
5. The student will dispose of trash in the proper container.	Have a couple of wastebaskets within close proximity for students to easily use without disturbing others at work. For example, one wastebasket can be in the back of the room while another is at the side of the room. At the end of each day, encourage students to check their desks and work areas for trash and to dispose of it properly.
6. The student will keep his desk and classroom possessions neat.	Have a regular time for students to check that their desks and possessions are neat and orderly. For example, every Wednesday morning and on Friday afternoons before school is out for the weekend, provide time for students to neaten their desks, organize folders, and check that their possessions, in general, are well taken care of. For older students who have lockers or other storage areas, allow them to check those places and neaten them up and organize them as needed.

Individual Objective	Strategy or Intervention
7. The student will clean up after breaking or spilling something.	Spills and breakage will occur often enough, so have clean-up materials easily available for students to use. Have paper towels and cleaners close by for spilled items. For broken items, have students signal to you that something needs to be cleaned so they are not injured in the process. You might encourage a student to bring you the broom or brush, the dustpan, and a bag for the broken items.
8. The student will respect others' care of the outdoor environment.	Arrange a project with your principal that your students can do to improve the school's outside environment. Students might plant trees, flowers, and shrubs in an area; paint signs or railings; or clean up an area. If possible, secure an ongoing project so students can practice caring for the environment. Older students might job shadow or help a groundskeeper. When students take pride in their own work, they're more likely to respect the hard work of others.
9. The student will learn to appreciate the outside environment.	Either via pictures or videos you take or by taking a bus tour around your area, show your students the beauty in their surroundings. As students observe, have them list what's been done to make a locale attractive and appealing. Discuss the effects of vandalism in a community, too, if it seems appropriate.

Eagle Point Park

1. New playground equipment
2. Park name planted in flowers
3. Resurfaced park roads
4. Creation of bike lane
5. Nature Center
6. Mississippi River Overlook

Individual Objective	Strategy or Intervention

▶ Handling Emergencies at School

1. The student will identify an accident or emergency situation.

Invite your school nurse, police liaison officer, or an outside health and safety person to discuss emergency situations with your students. Have the speakers tailor descriptions and discussions to the abilities of your students. Books and videos can be used to help illustrate each emergency. For older students, encourage them to join organizations like Scouts, Explorers, Junior Red Cross, and/or to take baby-sitting and water safety classes to learn more about handling emergencies as well as to learn about possible vocations in the field of rescue work.

2. The student will report an accident or emergency to the teacher or other appropriate adult.

Walk the student to areas in the school where he can report an emergency, like the nurse's office and the main office. If the student is in a class, he should be taught to immediately report an emergency to the teacher there even if he isn't sure it is an emergency. Discuss with the student the kinds of emergencies that can take place, like seizures, falls, exposures to chemicals, and accidents on the playground, during gym, or while waiting for buses to arrive.

Individual Objective	Strategy or Intervention
3. The student will know the difference between fire and tornado warnings.	First of all, make sure students can distinguish the warning sounds for each type of emergency. Enlist the help of the administration to play the sounds a couple of times just to listen and learn the difference between them. Then make separate signs for the room with descriptors of the sounds to help cue students. For example, perhaps the fire alarm sounds more like the warbling siren of an emergency vehicle while the tornado warning is a long blast. Imitate the sound for students and have them rehearse what to do.
4. The student will follow school rules and procedures for emergencies.	Have students make individual booklets for the rules and procedures for each emergency. Students can write the steps or rules to follow and then illustrate them. After completing each emergency booklet, practice and rehearse the rules, drills, and procedures with the students.

Fire Emergency

1. The fire alarm sounds.
2. Line up at the door quickly.
3. Walk quietly with your teacher and class out of the school building.
4. Move away from the building.
5. Stay with your teacher and classmates.

Individual Objective	Strategy or Intervention
5. The student will handle personal emergencies.	Inevitably students will forget to bring something to school, have to call a parent for something they need, or have an incident occur at school that needs handling. First of all, have the student and the parent fill out an information card that can be kept in the classroom with contact names and numbers in case of need or for emergencies. Also make the student aware of people in the building that he can turn to for help, like the school nurse, a guidance counselor, or office personnel. Let the student also know when and where he can make a phone call to a parent if needed.

Individual Objective	Strategy or Intervention
▶ Coping in the Lunchroom	
1. The student will be able to get his utensils and carry his tray to the table.	Prior to the student's first lunch at school, talk about the procedure, including paying for lunch, getting utensils and the lunch itself, and the clean-up process afterward. If possible, rehearse ahead of time in the actual lunchroom so the student is comfortable with the process and will be able to handle it when crowds of students are around.
2. The student will be able to use eating utensils properly.	Two problems may surface related to eating with utensils. First, the student may be used to using his hands or using utensils improperly and not having good, socially-acceptable manners. Second, the student may use the utensils to fight and get into arguments with other students seated with him. Whichever the case, arrange to sit at the student's table with him during lunch time to instruct him in proper use of utensils and behavior at the lunch table. If possible, also enlist the help of a favorite teacher or coach to sit at the table and alternate times with that person until the student knows how to act.
3. The student will be able to handle and eat his own food.	Restrict any student who eats food off others' trays or handles his own food inappropriately from sitting in the lunchroom for lunch. Make sure the student understands that there is a minimum of polite, respectful behavior required for him to join his peers at lunch. If needed, obtain a sack lunch for the student from the lunchroom or have him bring one from home and eat in the classroom until he's ready to join others in the lunchroom for lunch.

Individual Objective	Strategy or Intervention
4. The student will keep his food in his mouth.	Review meal time rules with your students prior to lunch time for the first week or so. Provide a sack lunch in another area for any student who is unable to exhibit the basic behaviors allowing him the privilege of eating with peers.
5. The student will dispose of unwanted food, paper, and utensils properly.	Initially circulate among your students or enlist the help of an assistant to see that students are not leaving food, trash, or utensils at the table and that they are properly disposing of them. Any student who is unable to follow the rule after a reminder or two needs to eat lunch in a separate location until he learns that cleaning up is his personal responsibility and no one else's.
6. The student will use a voice volume appropriate to a given situation. 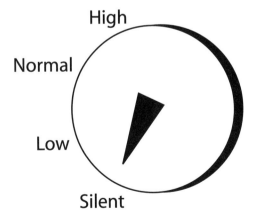 (reproducible full-size copy on page 154)	Develop a voice volume visual reminder to show students which voice volume is appropriate for the occasion. For example, you may allow a Normal voice volume level in the lunchroom, while a Silent (or Off) volume is acceptable in the library. Put the visual reminder on the chalkboard or overhead. Make individual copies for students who may need them at their desks. When needed, point to the visual reminder to regulate volume for the entire class or say something like, "Look at your voice volume reminder, Joel" to cue individual students.

Individual Objective	Strategy or Intervention

▶ Moving Around the School Environment

1. The student will be able to form and walk in a line.

   Have a consistent way of lining up students so they don't compete to be "first." For example, for one month, line up students going from the front rows in your seating chart to the back rows. The next month, reverse the order, back to front, so line order is fair. Exit the room only when students are quiet and in line.

2. The student will be able to find common locations around the school building.

   Rather than take a "grand tour" of the school building to orient students, take short, focused tours over several days during which students complete "assignments." For example, a student could be sent to the nurse to have his height and weight checked as part of a measurement unit in math while also learning where the nurse's office is.

3. The student will be able to identify his teacher's room number and name.

   Laminate a schedule card with room numbers, classes, and teacher names for the student. (You may want extras in case the cards get lost!) Make sure each teacher's room has the room number and name readily visible on it. Each day, the student brings the card and locates the room and teacher by referring to the card and making a "match."

Student _Justin_		
Room 104	Mr. Swords	Math
Room 120	Ms. Hart	Art (Tuesday, Thursday)
Big Gym	Mr. Jiminez	P.E. (Monday, Wednesday, Friday)
Room 106	Mrs. Belker	Language Arts
Room 125	Mr. Golden	Science
Room 138	Ms. Brown	Social Skills

Individual Objective	Strategy or Intervention
4. The student will enter the school building appropriately.	Prepare a rule sheet or list of expectations for entering the school building in the morning. Rules might include the following: • Walk when entering the building. • Check the time on the clock. • Go immediately to your room (locker). • Gather your materials for the day. Initially enlist the help of your administration in supervising the entrance to help students make an appropriate transition (if your school doesn't already do this).
5. The student will walk in the hall quietly and at a reasonable pace.	For quick "excess energy" breaks to help an overactive student to regain focus, let the student practice correct walking in the hallway for a few minutes. Provide the student with a destination within sight of the classroom. Then have the student practice correct walking there and back, quietly entering the classroom when he returns.
6. The student will enter the classroom and take his seat immediately.	Provide an incentive at the student's desk to motivate him to get seated. You might use ideas like the following: • positive notes about previous successes the day or period before • a favorite book • quiet, quick hands-on activity (e.g., small puzzle) • crosswords or word puzzles • pages to color and favorite markers • treat or piece of gum

Individual Objective	Strategy or Intervention
7. The student will return to his seat without disturbing others.	We all know the student who can't move about the classroom without brushing by and upsetting a classmate or swiping an item off a desk for attention as he returns to his seat. Eliminate such temptations for the student by selecting a seat and a specific route for movement. With the student, practice a "safe," consistent route that you expect the student to follow as he legitimately moves about the classroom. For the student to be allowed movement, he must use this path and should ask permission before moving unless given specific direction to do so.
8. The student will be able to locate classroom materials and equipment.	Place materials and equipment in a consistent spot in the room so students know where to get them. Make the location a place where students pass by as few other students as possible so they are not distracting or disrupting others. You may also want to put your homework bin for collecting completed assignments in the same area to help students remember what's due. Seeing what other students have turned in serves as a visual reminder.
9. The student will follow safety rules when crossing streets. **Crossing Rules** 1. Cross only at the crosswalks. 2. Obey any crossing guards, crosswalk signs, and markings. 3. Look both ways. 4. Walk quickly to the other side.	Develop a short rule list for a student to refer to in learning how to cross the street safely. Provide a copy for parents, too, so they can practice with the student and reinforce what he's learning. If a student is crossing near school, arrange for a good role model or a parent to accompany the student initially to and from school.

Individual Objective	Strategy or Intervention
10. The student will be able to locate and get on the school bus on time.	Some students, particularly those with more organization and time awareness difficulties, may need extra time to prepare for getting to the bus on time. Allow these students a few extra minutes to gather materials and belongings in the classroom or to go to their lockers to get organized for the bus and the evening. To remember which bus to take and where to get it, have the student post an index card with the place and bus number in his locker or inside his desk as a reminder.
11. The student will follow safety rules on the bus and exhibit appropriate bus behavior.	Rather than having random seating on the bus, ask the bus driver to have regular assigned seats for students. Work with the driver to have the student seated near a good behavioral role model, preferably toward the front of the bus until he can learn and apply bus safety rules and display appropriate bus behavior.

Improving Interpersonal Skills

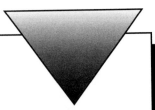

How many times a day do your students interact with someone else? All day long, right? Interaction is inevitable: at home before school, on the bus, in the school hallways, in the classroom, during lunch, with friends after school, with an employer at an after-school job, and with parents and siblings at night. For our students to succeed in school and life, they must have a wide range of social and interpersonal skills to help them interact with a variety of people in a variety of situations.

Many students with behavior disorders have social interaction problems because they've never actually learned appropriate skills. Their social problems occur due to a deficit in social skills rather than an inability or refusal to learn the skills. These students need direct instruction in how to perceive social situations and which social skills to use in what circumstances.

Students with behavior disorders need to acquire and practice interpersonal skills in the following areas:

- accepting authority
- coping with conflict
- gaining attention
- helping self and others
- socializing and making conversation
- participating in organized play and activities
- playing informally
- developing empathy and understanding
- showing respect for property

The objectives, strategies, and interventions in this chapter will help your students acquire the interpersonal skills they need to interact appropriately with a variety of people in a variety of situations.

Yearly Goal: to improve relationships with peers, teachers, and others

Individual Objective	Strategy or Intervention
▶ **Accepting Authority**	
1. The student will interact appropriately with teachers.	Learning how to interact with teachers is a trial-and-error process for many students. From the first day of class, be sure that students know how to address you and know what basic respectful behaviors you want them to have toward you and each other in class. Let them know that you welcome their interactions with you. Give them concrete examples of when it's okay to interact socially (e.g., not in the middle of discussion, but as they walk into class is fine) and what topics are okay to discuss. If a student chooses an inappropriate time or topic to discuss, consistently respond "Now is not the appropriate time" and discuss the situation privately later on.
2. The student will know and follow classroom rules.	Establish politeness and respect for one another and for the adult in authority as part of your regular classroom rules. Post a short list of rules several places around the room to remind your students each day. The list on the left establishes respect as a theme for guiding students' behavior toward adults, peers, and property.

Classroom Rules of Respect

1. **Respect the adult in charge.**
   Look, listen, and cooperate.

2. **Respect each other.**
   Use "please" and "thank you."

3. **Respect your classroom.**
   Take care of the room and materials in it.

(reproducible full-size copy on page 155)

Individual Objective	Strategy or Intervention
3. The student will recognize the adult in authority.	Each time a student enters a new situation, be sure that she knows which adult is in authority. Formally introduce the student to the adult so she becomes familiar with who she should respect in the situation and who may help her. For example, in the library, the student may need to ask for permission or help from the librarian or a library assistant. Waiting outside for a bus to arrive, the student may need to listen to another teacher or a vice principal.
4. The student will comply with requests from adults in authority.	The student will deal with a variety of adults in authority throughout the school year. For example, people from the community might volunteer in classrooms or students might have substitute teachers. Whenever possible, prepare students for times when there will be a different adult in charge. Tell the students you expect the adult to be treated with the respect given any other familiar adult in school.
5. The student will be able to ask permission of an authority figure.	With each new situation the student encounters, she will need to know under what circumstances she must ask permission and who to ask. Prepare students ahead of time by presenting problem-solving situations. Write each situation on a card with examples of times the students would need to ask permission. The students can then rehearse asking permission with you.

Problem-solving Situation: You're on a field trip to the local park. You have to go to the bathroom.

Supervising Adults: Your teacher and volunteer parents

What do you do?

Who do you ask?

Individual Objective	Strategy or Intervention
6. The student will be able to accept "no" for an answer.	Have a discussion with the student about when an adult or other person in authority may need to say "no." Explain that adults don't make these decisions arbitrarily. Circumstances for refusing permission may include situations like the following: • to protect the student's safety • the student has not earned the privilege • it's another student's turn • the timing of the request isn't good When a student asks permission and is told "no," be consistent in presenting one of the above circumstances as your reasoning so the student can accept the answer.

► **Coping with Conflict**

1. The student will be able to express displeasure verbally in an appropriate manner.	Let a student who is expressing herself inappropriately know immediately. Discuss with the student what happens when she expresses displeasure in inappropriate ways. Emphasize in particular how she is perceived by others and how others are likely to react. Use examples like the ones on the left to help illustrate. Then discuss better ways to handle displeasure.

Coping with Conflict (Student-Teacher)

Situation 1	Teacher has just assigned a long-term project for a class
Student Reaction	"This sucks! I hate doing projects!"
Teacher Reaction	May view the student as uncooperative and lazy. Consequently he may be less helpful to student with such strong feelings.
Better Student Reaction	"Projects are hard! I'm going to need help with this."
Teacher Reaction	Will help the student get started after delivering main directions to class.

(reproducible full-size copy on page 156)

Coping with Conflict (Student-Peer)

Situation 2	Another student is making a suggestion for a game to play during gym class.
Student Reaction	"That's a stupid game! There's no challenge to it."
Peer Reactions	Avoid student who puts their ideas down. Student likely won't be chosen for a team because she comes across as a whiner and poor sport.
Better Student Reaction	"Cool. That's a fun game" or "How about playing Pickle instead? Then more people can play."

(reproducible full-size copy on page 157)

Individual Objective	Strategy or Intervention
2. The student will know how and when to apologize.	Provide face-saving ways for students to apologize. For example, the student might learn to say "I'm sorry. That won't happen again" or you might allow the student to write an apology. Once the apology occurs, tell the student the incident has been dealt with and won't be brought up again.
3. The student will ignore teasing or name calling.	Many commercial videos are available as well as children's literature books about the subject of teasing and name calling. Contact your local area education agency representative as well your school psychologist, school social worker, and school librarian for appropriate materials. Since teasing and name calling are prevalent behaviors among children, use the materials and discuss the topics often.
4. The student will be able to leave or to call for adult help when physically assaulted.	Coach students to immediately go to "safe" people when their safety has been threatened by another student. Have three safe people the student can go to, like his school counselor, the vice principal, or another teacher. Remind students that if they retaliate, right or wrong, they too may face school or legal consequences. If possible, the student should leave the situation immediately and seek help.
5. The student will be able to walk away from anger-provoking situations.	Provide a place for a student to go to when she begins to feel overwhelmed and/or angered by a situation. For example, you might allow the student to walk to the back of the room to peruse books or look at a bulletin board to give her some "breathing room" or to step outside the room for a couple of minutes to regain control.

Individual Objective	Strategy or Intervention
6. The student will be able to express anger with non-aggressive words.	First teach students the concept of aggressive words and behavior: very strong, emotional words that make someone feel like fighting back. Then role-play to illustrate the difference between the impact of aggressive words and the impact of "neutral" or non-aggressive words when used to express anger. You might put short scripts on index cards for the students to choose from and role-play, followed by a discussion of the language that created an aggressive response. Let students make up their own role-play scripts for more practice.

Situation 1: Sean has borrowed Josh's pencil without asking. Josh wants the pencil back.

Josh: "Hey, jerk, who said you could take that? Give it back!!!!!"

Aggressive? Nonaggressive?

What do you think Sean will say? What do you think will happen next? Why? Act out your ideas after you discuss the questions.

Situation 2: Sean has borrowed Josh's pencil without asking. Josh wants the pencil back.

Josh: "Hey, Sean, did you ask to borrow my pencil? Please ask me next time, okay? I don't like people to borrow things without asking me."

Aggressive? Nonaggressive?

What do you think Sean will say? What do you think will happen next? Why? Act out your ideas after you discuss the questions.

7. The student will be able to handle constructive criticism or punishment appropriately.	Provide constructive criticism privately to a student, like after class or by writing comments on a sheet of paper. The student will be better able to focus on the suggestions themselves rather than his feelings about being "corrected." Deal with any punishment or negative consequences after class when the student can save face and the class won't be needlessly distracted.

Individual Objective	Strategy or Intervention
8. The student will be able to handle negative feelings like anger and frustration appropriately.	Some students will need to learn anger-management strategies, especially if their anger or outbursts of frustration distract and agitate others. First, invite your school psychologist, guidance counselor, social worker, or other individual who can do anger-management training to observe your students within the classroom. Next, discuss together what behavior patterns were observed and what needs the student may have. Then have students regularly meet individually or in small groups with the school psychologist to learn how to manage their anger. Be sure that students' parents consent to training so they can help with any follow-up activities or behavioral reinforcement at home.
9. The student will be able to resolve conflict situations.	Provide the student with a step-by-step strategy for solving a conflict independently. For example, on a "strategy card," list the steps the student should use to solve a problem. In individual sessions with the student, practice the steps with realistic, theoretical situations using the Problem-Solving Tips (PST) card. Praise the student for attempting to apply the steps. Then encourage the student to use the problem-solving strategy steps to solve her own conflicts.

 Pose the problem. State the conflict in just a few words.

 Scan through your choices. Think of at least three ways the conflict might be handled.

 Take action. Think through the possible effects of each choice. Take action with the choice that best solves the conflict.

(reproducible full-size copy on page 158)

| 10. The student will refrain from fighting or being aggressive with other students. | At the beginning of the school year (and/or semester), each teacher should go over school rules regarding aggressive behavior for all students in her class. They should discuss and give examples of aggressive types of behavior, including verbal and physical assaults. Teachers also need to describe the consequences for the different levels of aggressive behavior as indicated in their school rule books. Then each teacher needs to be very observant and consistent in handling and preventing any behaviors that may escalate to aggression. |

Individual Objective	Strategy or Intervention

▶ Gaining Attention

1. The student will know when to use "please" and "thank you."

Honor requests only when the student uses "please" in a request such as "May I please use the restroom?" or "Do you have a pencil I might use, please?" When the request is honored, she should be expected to say "thank you" or "thanks" before you respond "you're welcome." Some students may need to role-play how to make such requests, especially when they first become members of your class. Expecting politeness usually leads to a calmer, more patient, respectful environment.

2. The student will raise her hand in class to gain the teacher's attention.

Be consistent in how you recognize students, whether it's during discussion, while they're volunteering for something, or if a student is wanting something. Excited, enthusiastic, or more impulsive students may shout out your name while hands are frantically waving. Recognize only those students who are calmly raising their hands. For a student who is particularly impulsive but who is appropriately raising his hand, you might say his name or stop near his desk and say, "Marques, I'll be with you in a couple minutes. Thank you for waiting patiently."

3. The student will be able to wait to be recognized before speaking out.

Create a class poster and individual posters to put at students' desks for students who need turn-taking rule reminders. When the student speaks out before being recognized, remind her of the guidelines for discussion.

Discussion Guidelines

1. Raise your hand.

2. Wait patiently for the teacher to call on you.

3. Give your ideas or answer.

4. Say, "I'm done" to show that someone else can now talk.

(reproducible full-size copy on page 159)

Individual Objective	Strategy or Intervention
4. The student will recognize the need to share time and attention with others.	The student with a behavior disorder may need concrete parameters set for her when sharing time and attention with others. For example, the student may be working in the library researching a topic for a science report and request your help, but you're busy with other students. You may give the student a specific time when you will get to her or once you are helping her, you may tell her you have 10 minutes to provide help. For example, if the student is vying for attention during a class discussion, you can focus her by saying "Pam, I will let you speak after John and Ty."
5. The student will be able to ask for help appropriately from teachers without gaining undue attention from others.	For the particularly impulsive or noisy student, you will need to set specific parameters for seeking help. Determine if the student should ask for help from her seat or if she may get up to ask for help. One possible way to alleviate undue attention is to check in with the student when she first begins an assignment or activity to see that things are going okay. Then periodically check in with the student's progress along the way, praising her for appropriate behavior.
6. The student will be able to gain peer attention in appropriate ways.	As part of the rules for your classroom, set parameters for appropriate ways for students to get their peers' attention. The most appropriate way is to say the other student's name and politely interrupt in order to express what they want. Poking or rough housing with another student or taking the student's materials should not be accepted as ways to get attention as students may not always understand "limits" to attention-seeking or aggressive behavior.

Individual Objective	Strategy or Intervention
7. The student will be able to ask peers for help.	When students work independently in class, allow them to help one another as long as they follow rules and expectations. Rules like the following can help students behave appropriately during independent work time. • Ask the teacher permission to get help from another student. • Work quietly together. • Limit the "help" time to 5 minutes or less. • Return quietly to your desk.
8. The student will be able to offer help to peers.	Provide plenty of partnering activities in and out of the classroom so students have more practice interacting with each other and with being helpful to one another. For example, a student with behavioral difficulties may have very strong math skills. Allow that student to work with another student who needs help in math. If possible, let the partners turn in a joint assignment for full credit.
9. The student will be cooperative while participating in learning groups.	When putting students together in cooperative learning groups, provide good role models for the student with behavioral difficulties. Assign roles for each group member so that responsibilities are clear. For example, if students are completing a social studies assignment, one student might be the note taker, one student might be responsible for any drawings or illustrations, and another student might be responsible for the actual presentation of the project.

Individual Objective	Strategy or Intervention
10. The student will be able to seek help without whining or complaining.	Establish a predetermined time expectation for the student to attempt to work independently. Tell the student she must try to do the work on her own at first. During the given time, the student may not make negative comments (e.g., whine, complain, blame) or do other things to avoid attempting the work independently. If needed, set a kitchen timer to help the student focus. After the given time, provide help to the student.
11. The student will understand the concepts of positive and negative behaviors.	Provide the student with a basic definition of positive and negative behaviors. • Kind behaviors make someone smile. When you are kind to someone, you are acting in a positive way. • Unkind behaviors make someone frown. When you are unkind to someone, you are acting in a negative way. Or • Positive behaviors add to someone's happiness in some way. • Negative behaviors take away someone's happiness in some way. Give the students samples of behaviors to label good or disrespectful/bad, or positive or negative. Once a student seems to understand, apply those terms to the student's own behaviors, largely praising to help shape positive behaviors.

Individual Objective	Strategy or Intervention
12. The student will be able to distinguish between positive and negative behaviors.	Develop lists of positive and negative behaviors with your students. Then discuss the different effects that positive and negative behaviors have on relationships with others.

Positive Behavior	Effect
listening politely	others will want to talk to you
using "please" and "thank you"	others will want to share with you or help you
helping someone else	others will help you when you need it

Negative Behavior	Effect
interrupting rudely	others will ignore you in conversation
taking things from others	others will hide their things and not share
blurting answers in class	others won't be able to hear or learn.

(reproducible full-size copy on page 160)

As needed and as a student is open to it, remind the student of her positive behaviors. Enlist her help in working on any negative behavior by emphasizing what she has to gain from it personally in her relationship with others (e.g., how it will help her get along better with others and/or how much more others will like her).

Individual Objective	Strategy or Intervention
13. The student will learn ways to acknowledge praise and positive attention.	Make politeness a requirement in your classroom along with keeping the focus on making positive remarks. A simple "thank you" for a helpful act or cooperation by you or another student can eventually develop into comments like "Rich, you did a great job of organizing the papers for me. Thanks." Don't get too emotive or overly complimentary as students may think comments are insincere or manipulative rather than appreciative.
14. The student will be able to make appropriate physical contact with others.	Teachers are excellent role models for showing students appropriate ways to make physical contact. When a student does well on an assignment or presentation, the teacher can walk over and shake the student's hand and say "good job" or give the student a "high five." As students enter your classroom each day, shake their hands "hello" or give them "high fives" or verbal praise for previous good work or good behavior.

Individual Objective	Strategy or Intervention
15. The student will not provoke or interfere with other students.	Give students very specific times and guidelines for when and how they may interact with other students. For example, if students are to work in pairs, you might say, "You may work only with one other person. You are to stay in your work area and finish the assignment. I will tell you when you can share your work with someone else." If a student attempts to interfere or provoke others, remind her of the rules for interacting in this instance. Any student who cannot handle work with a partner, even with such concrete direction, may need to work individually until appropriate skills are developed.
16. The student will be able to accept friendly teasing.	Work with students to be able to distinguish between friendly teasing and hurtful teasing. Explain that friendly teasing happens because someone actually likes you, while the other kind is meant to make you feel bad. Discuss contrasting examples like the ones on the left by putting them on index cards the students can draw from and then discuss. Have students also come up with their own examples. (Be sure to include examples where the tone used or the way someone says something is how the teasing is occurring.) Encourage students to come to you when they are teased rather than react to other students if they are unsure about the kind of teasing.

Friendly Teasing	"Oh, are you going to hit that ball out of the park like you did last time?"
Hurtful Teasing	"Teron is up to bat. Guess we'd better get ready to take the field!"

Friendly Teasing	"Hey, Shaun, can we borrow that wild shirt of yours for Hawaiian Day?"
Hurtful Teasing	"What did you do? Pull your clothes out of the hamper this morning?"

Individual Objective	Strategy or Intervention

17. The student will not make inappropriate comments or noises in the classroom.

Behavior Observation Chart

Name Drew Reynolds   Date Tuesday, November 12

Class Reading Class

Teacher Mrs. Rose

Behavior Observed	Number of Times
Made strange noises	//// /
Made rude comments to others	////

(reproducible full-size copy on page 161)

Before a student can work on controlling inappropriate comments or noises, she needs to be made aware of what she's doing and how often she's doing it. First, without letting the student know it, observe the type and number of inappropriate incidences per given period of time (e.g., during one class period). Record the type and number of incidences with tally marks on a chart like the one on the left. Then let the student know what you've observed. Next provide a tally sheet for both the student and yourself to record the number of incidences during a given time period over several days. Later, compare results and problem solve together how the student can act more appropriately. Sometimes raising awareness is enough to stop a problem, while other times contingency and reward plans need to be developed.

You might ask other teachers to make observations as well to see if there's any pattern to the inappropriate behavior or if it occurs more or less in given classes or during certain situations.

18. The student will refrain from interrupting the teacher.

Develop a signal or phrase that lets all students (especially those most apt to interrupt) know when you are done speaking or giving directions. You might say, "I'm done with what I have to tell you. Thank you for listening carefully. Now, does anyone have questions or need anything?" Use the same phrase every time to train students who otherwise don't pick up well on verbal cues.

Individual Objective	Strategy or Intervention
19. The student will be able to compliment others. 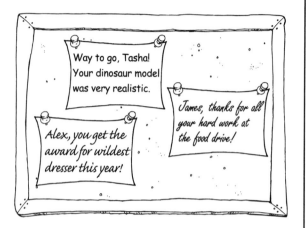	Make a bulletin board in the classroom where examples of compliments can be displayed. Be sure compliments range from comments about clothing to praise for helpfulness and recognition of talents. Personalize compliments if possible. Encourage students to create their own compliments to add to the board and change the display frequently.
20. The student will practice good manners.	Insist on good manners in your classroom and other areas of the school building. Use "please" and "thank you" when students cooperate with your instructions. Coach students to tell people like the lunchroom staff "thank you" when served or when paying for their meal.

Individual Objective	Strategy or Intervention

▶ Greeting Others

1. The student will make and maintain eye contact when spoken to.

   Make sure that you and other teachers or adults in the student's life speak and continue speaking to the student only when he is maintaining eye contact with you. Let other teachers and adults know this is a particular skill the student is working on. A consistency of expectations shared and modeled by all those who interact with the student will help the student learn this important social interaction skill.

2. The student will respond to her name.

   Some students need to be taught how to respond to someone calling their names. Have the student simply practice saying "Yes?" when her name is spoken. That indicates she's listening for what will follow. It's a neutral response and may prevent students lapsing into bad habits like saying "Huh?" or "What?" which may not necessarily sound inviting or cooperative.

3. The student will state her name when asked.

   A student will need to be able to state her name for a variety of reasons, from identifying who she is in a class and what she prefers to be called, to providing her name for her driver's permit. For the classroom, the student might say, "I'm Jennifer Delavan. I like to be called Jenny." For formal purposes, the same student may need to say, "I'm Jennifer Erin Delavan" and even spell out her name. Encourage the student to always make eye contact so she can assess whether her message was heard as well as to show interest and make a favorable impression.

Individual Objective	Strategy or Intervention
4. The student will greet adults and peers by name.	Stand outside your room each class period so you can greet students individually as they enter. Require students to greet you back in response. Stick with a variety of only two or three ways of greeting so more hesitant students can learn and practice. For example, you might say, "Hi, Jake. How's your day going so far?" or "Good afternoon, Melissa. Did you have a good lunch today?"
5. The student will be able to introduce herself to others.	Have your students practice making introductions to the significant adults in the building. Introductions will serve two purposes: to familiarize your students with adults who may be helpful to them, and to allow the significant adults to meet each student in a positive manner. Have your students introduce themselves to adults including guidance counselors, the school psychologist, the principal and vice principal, school nurse, librarian, and lunchroom staff.
6. The student will be able to introduce two people to each other.	Put students in charge of introducing their parents or other family members who attend school functions like an IEP meeting or an open house. Practice with the student before the event takes place. Then have the student be the first to make the introductions.

Individual Objective	Strategy or Intervention

▶ Helping Self and Others

1. The student will be able to help teachers and adults when asked.

Most students like positive recognition for helping out in a situation. Encourage other adults to ask the student for help frequently, even if they're not sure how the student will react initially. A student may be given the responsibility of getting equipment out during gym class or helping to put chairs up at the end of the day. Make sure the student receives specific directions about how to help so she doesn't get frustrated. After a while, the student is likely to look for opportunities to help out on her own.

2. The student will help her peers when asked.

Pair students for class duties or assignments. Be sure to place the student with a behavior disorder with a student who is a good behavioral role model but also who can learn academically from the student with a behavior disorder. Arrange for the same pairs to work together frequently so they can form a partnership in which their abilities complement one another and they can learn how beneficial it is to help one another.

3. The student will be able to offer help to others voluntarily.

Get to know the strengths and abilities of the student. When opportunities arise to offer help, coach the student to volunteer. For example, if the student has artistic talents, she might offer to make the drawings for a class time line project in social studies. Eventually the student will begin to offer help on her own because she enjoys the positive feelings and recognition she gains from her peers and adults.

Individual Objective	Strategy or Intervention
4. The student will be able to ask for a favor.	Students may occasionally need to borrow some lunch money or other materials from another student, or they may need to ask another student for specific help, like a ride to school. Determine ahead of time what rules for borrowing or asking favors you want to establish in your classroom so students don't take advantage of each other. If needed, offer to problem solve with students if any conflict arises from a situation.
5. The student will be able to accept advice or help from others.	For all of your students, request that they ask another student first before offering help or advice. They might say things like "I think I can help you with that, May I help you?" or "I can share some advice with you that has worked for me." Encourage them not to jump in and do something for someone or to take over without permission. Model such behavior and requests yourself so the classroom becomes a respectful, helpful, supportive environment.

► Socializing and Making Conversation

1. The student will be able to listen and attend to another person talking.	Teach the student about body language that shows when someone is listening and attentive. The student should make eye contact with the individual and listen without talking until the other person is done talking. Encourage the student to try to ask a follow-up question related to what the person was saying.

Individual Objective	Strategy or Intervention
2. The student will speak in a tone of voice and with a volume appropriate to the situation.  Talk in a conversational tone. Don't shout across the lunchroom. (reproducible blank copy on page 162)	Have students make illustrated posters or small books describing the appropriate voice tone and volume for a given situation. Then have students share their posters and/or books with the rest of the class. Post and put their illustrations around the room as reminders.
3. The student will wait her turn in a conversation.	Some students may need guided practice and cueing signals to know how to take turns in conversations. Encourage a speaker in a conversation to say, "I'm done. Does anyone else want to say something?" as a concrete verbal cue. Or, if the teacher is present, she and the student can agree on a signal ahead of time, like a nod from the teacher, to know when to enter a conversation.
4. The student will make relevant remarks in conversations with peers.	Make conversation a game. A couple of times a week, have student pairs have short conversations. Provide the pair with the topic of conversation, like sports events, music, clothing, TV shows, parents, a current event, or work. Or let pairs draw a card with a topic out of a box. Allow 5-10 minutes for the conversation. At the end of the conversation, have each partner summarize individually in writing what was discussed. They should also record any irrelevant comments and what happened as a result, like getting confused or feeling angry because they might not have felt listened to.

Individual Objective	Strategy or Intervention
5. The student will initiate conversations with adults in informal situations.	Invite other adults to your classroom frequently to work with and interact with your students. For example, you might invite parents, school volunteers, guidance counselors, the school psychologist, speech-language pathologist, the principal and vice principal, school nurse, librarian, and lunchroom staff to take part in lesson activities from time to time so students can practice all kinds of social skills like conversations and introductions with adults.
6. The student will make relevant remarks in conversations with adults.	Encourage adults who are around your students to remind them if their comments are inappropriate or irrelevant during conversations. Have the adults use consistent ways of describing the comments. For example, an adult might say, "That's personal information and should be kept to yourself" or "Please make comments that have to do with what we're talking about."
7. The student will initiate appropriate conversation with peers in informal situations.	Make sure the student has an opportunity to be around peers in informal situations where conversation might occur. For example, allow free time in the classroom for students to play or interact, or make sure a student is around peers in the lunch room so she can learn appropriate conversational skills. Talk with the student ahead of time about topics she might bring up for discussion.

Individual Objective	Strategy or Intervention
8. The student will be able to join an on-going conversation. *Example:* Ricki: What are you doing after school? Matt: I dunno. I might go to the park and play some hoops. Ricki: Can I come? I can get my bike and meet you there. Matt: Okay, I'll see you there.	Joining a conversation requires two key skills: listening closely and entering a conversation at an appropriate pausing point. Tape record sample conversations with the help of other students. Then have the student listen, pausing the tape at a key spot. Have the student paraphrase what the conversation is about. Let the student then propose what she might say to join the conversation. Be sure to include a sample conversation that is more private in nature so the student can learn there are times when she should not join an on-going conversation.
9. The student will be able to appropriately exit a conversation.	Remind the student that wandering away from a conversation without helping to end it may make a peer think she is disinterested, unfriendly, or possibly angry about something. Teach the student some standard phrases to use, like "See you after school, I'll talk to you later," or something specific and appropriate, like "Good luck at your game tonight."
10. The student will be able to ignore the interruptions of others.	When a student is tempted to react to an interruption, steer the conversation back on track with a follow-up question related to the topic. Praise the student afterward by saying, "Thank you for keeping your mind on what you were saying to the rest of us. You were describing something very interesting."

Individual Objective	Strategy or Intervention
11. The student will make appropriate conversation with other students.	To make conversation, students have to be able to learn about each other's likes, dislikes, hobbies, and activities. As a routine part of class work or activities, have students do quick peer interviews. For example, if a science class is learning about amphibians, student pairs could share the first time they saw or handled a frog or salamander.
12. The student will be able to refrain from tattling.	Some students tattle as a way of getting social attention from their peers or extra attention from the teacher. Initially, privately conference with the student to see if there is an actual problem to be solved. If so, bring the students with the conflict together and have them attempt to solve the problem. Once the student knows that the "issue" that provoked the tattling will be addressed directly with her peers, she will either learn to resolve the conflict on her own or may hesitate to tattle again. Refrain from settling a student's peer problems for her and consistently remind her to problem solve the situation herself before requesting help from you.
13. The student will interact appropriately with peers.	You will need to provide direct instruction on appropriate interactions each time a student interacts with peers until the student generalizes such skills herself. Skill instruction will also need to fit each kind of situation or setting in which the interaction might occur. For example, if a student wants to join a group of students in the lunch room, she needs to first determine if there is room for her at the table. She also needs to learn to say something like "Is it okay if I sit at your table?" Review the skills prior to the student going to lunch each day until it becomes automatic for her.

Individual Objective	Strategy or Intervention
14. The student will show respect for others' "space."	Establish a "space" rule in your classroom. When students are standing and conversing, the rule may be to maintain a distance of 18 inches or so in front of you and on each side. When students are working in pairs, you may require that a distance of one foot be kept between their materials and their bodies so they aren't crowding each other. You will need to repeat the rule routinely as well as adapt a "space" rule to each situation or activity as it occurs. Also, during work or activities, circulate and monitor whether students are following the rule.
15. The student will be able to make and maintain a friendship.	Friendships are often based on sharing mutual interests. Set up interest centers for students to work and play in when given free time. For example, one interest center might be for playing board games, another for working with art materials, or another for interactive computer games. Or have a during or after-school volunteer project where students can work and get to know each other in a different way and explore interests.

▶ **Participating in Organized Play and Activities**

1. The student will follow rules when playing games.	Before a student participates in a game, make sure she understands the rules. Write the rules on a sheet of paper the student can review before playing. Check to see that the student understands the rules. For example, if the student is learning a new game in PE class, encourage the teacher to let you know ahead of time. Then you can review the rules with the student prior to class time.

Individual Objective	Strategy or Intervention
	Even if a student already knows "how" to play a game, reviewing the rules ahead of time is a good idea as part of establishing expectations for behavior and game playing.
2. The student will wait her turn when playing games.	If a student has trouble waiting her turn, stick with games she is familiar with and is capable of playing without difficulty. If possible, just have a small group of students play so the student only has to wait a short time. This will also give her plenty of opportunity to get used to the routine of turn taking. Once the student acquires turn-taking skills, allow her to move on to more challenging games.
3. The student will be comfortable playing competitive games.	Whether it's a board game, a gym game with equipment, or a game outside during recess, provide a variety of choices for students. Choices should include things like variety in number of players, complexity of rules, difficulty of motor and coordination skills needed, and length of time to play. Hopefully the student will then choose something she feels most comfortable and confident playing.

Individual Objective	Strategy or Intervention
4. The student will willingly congratulate the winner in competitive games and activities.	Whenever you play a class game, practice congratulating the winner(s). An easy way is to have the rest of the class applaud or shake the winners' hands. Then, when the student plays in PE class or on a sports team, she knows the kinds of gracious and supportive behavior expected.
5. The student will be able to accept defeat in a positive way.	Learning about graciousness and the importance of showing good sportsmanship are worthwhile life-long skills to build into your daily curriculum for students of any age. Create curriculum-related activities that focus on the positives of competition and how it promotes trying one's best. Discuss how these concepts relate to everyday life whether it's playing a game on the playground, competition between sports teams, or several people vying for the same honor or position on the job. You might show (age- and content-appropriate) films about accepting defeat (e.g., *The Mighty Ducks, Hoosiers, Save the Last Dance, Finding Forrester*) and then follow with a class discussion.
6. The student will be able to share possessions and materials with others.	Allow the student to initially make her own choice with whom she's willing to share possessions and materials (for younger students, you might call these their "sharing partners" or "buddies"). Group the student with those peers with whom she's comfortable for activities and work assignments. As the student learns to trust individual peers, she'll be more willing to move into other groups and share with others.

Individual Objective	Strategy or Intervention
7. The student will be able to take turns in group activities.	Arrange ahead of time how students will be grouped together and how they'll take turns in group activities. Make the arrangement for a time period, like a week, so students will be able to predict when they take turns. Switch the arrangement for the next week so someone else gets to be first and second.

Turn-Taking Record Sheet

Group ___1___   Week _September 9-13_____

Activity _Spelling Computer Drill_____

	Dates				
Order of Turns	9/9	9/10	9/11	9/12	9/13
First Marcella	✓	✓	✓		
Second James	✓	✓			
Third Kasey	✓	✓			
Fourth Komal	✓	✓			
Fifth Lynn	✓				

(reproducible full-size copy on page 163)

A small record sheet can be helpful for students who need visual reminders. The more impulsive student might be put in charge of recording turn taking as a way to better direct her energy. Keeping consistent groups for the week and sometimes from one week to another may also facilitate development of interpersonal and teamwork skills.

▶ **Playing Informally**

1. The student will be able to play cooperatively with others.

Some students with behavior disorders may lack the social skills and comfort level or confidence required to interact with larger groups of students. However, they may be comfortable playing with two or three other students. During available "play time," like on the playground during recess, during classroom free time, or in a gym class, divide students into groups of two or three for games by counting off. A choice of appropriate activities could then be available for these small groups, like card games, shooting baskets, or jump rope. Depending on the length of the activity period, students could be signaled to "switch" to another activity with the same group partway through.

Individual Objective	Strategy or Intervention
2. The student will be able to ask appropriately to be included in play or a game or sport.	Before a play or activity session, ask the student what kinds of things she might like to do during that time. Rehearse with her how to ask to join in if she chooses a group activity. She might learn to ask by saying "Do you mind if I join your team?" or "Is it okay if I play the game too?"
3. The student will be able to share toys and equipment.	Expect the student to share toys and equipment a majority of the time. However, once a week, for example, allow her to have a no-share day. That day, she can choose a toy or piece of equipment to use the entire activity time. Chances are the novelty of the "privilege" will wear off and she'll prefer to share with others anyway.
4. The student will be able to accept the reasonable wishes of a play group.	During group play time, set a specific length of time for the student to interact cooperatively even if the game or activity isn't of her own choosing. For example, start with expecting 10 minutes of cooperative play, and eventually lengthen it to 20 minutes or so. Reward the student with an extra privilege for her positive interaction.
5. The student will be able to suggest an activity for the group to play.	Allow students to take turns suggesting and/or planning group activities. For example, for a recess period, five students in a class could arrange the activities for one day that week. Students might organize a "ball playing day" where kick ball, basketball, and four square are offered. Students must gather and return needed equipment. The next week, another group of five students can do the organizing and planning.

Individual Objective	Strategy or Intervention

▶ Developing Empathy and Understanding

1. The student will be sympathetic and empathetic to others' needs or feelings.

   Students with behavior disorders often have difficulty relating directly to others' needs and feelings because they often have difficulty expressing their own needs and feelings. Provide regular opportunities for these students to express their feelings in neutral situations. For example, as part of daily lesson plans, frequently read stories and view videos that may provoke a variety of feelings in your students. Then have them react to what they read or saw with a variety of expressive activities (e.g., write a letter to a character giving advice on a problem or draw or paint how she'd feel if she faced the situation in the movie). Students can share their reactions when appropriate.

2. The student will develop and practice tolerance and sensitivity for others with different abilities and characteristics.

   Explain to students that "tolerance" is understanding and accepting others' differences. Be sure students understand many ways individuals can be different—physically, educationally, religiously, ethnically, and so on. For any new situation in which a student's tolerance and sensitivity might be challenged, prepare her ahead of time so she can handle the situation appropriately. For example, if you have invited a speaker from another country to speak to your class, explain how the speaker may look and talk differently than your student might expect.

Individual Objective	Strategy or Intervention
3. The student will be able to express concern for another in acceptable ways.	Be sure to praise a student who shows concern for another even if she doesn't show it the appropriate way. Follow up by providing alternative behavior choices she can use the next time. For each choice, ask her how she would feel if someone showed concern for her in this manner. Encouraging her to put herself in another's place may help her better anticipate others' reactions.
4. The student will be able to perceive and identify others' feelings.	Weekly or daily, share news and magazine articles of human interest, locally, nationally, and world-wide. Have your students put themselves "in the shoes" of those in the articles and reflect how they might feel in those circumstances. You might have students write their responses in a journal.
5. The student will act in a way that acknowledges the feelings of others.	When handling interactions of any type between students, rather than make assumptions about how they feel or why they did what they did, ask them open-ended questions to elicit their feelings. You can say, "How do you feel about this?" or "Are you okay with the way things are going?" Frequently acknowledge your own feelings about things in your classroom and community so you serve as a role model. Many times students need to get in touch with their own feelings before they can understand or acknowledge someone else's feelings.

Individual Objective	Strategy or Intervention
6. The student will be able to keep a secret.	Secrets need to be respected and preserved for friendships. Play "What would happen if?" games often with the student to show her the consequences of secret-sharing. Use "What would happen if?" questions like the following: • What would happen if you told a friend about a surprise party planned for her? • What would happen if you told someone a secret your best friend had asked you to keep? • What would happen if you shared family information your parents asked you not to share?
7. The student will be able to diplomatically make a suggestion.	When students are asked to give suggestions, give them diplomatic suggestion-starting phrases to use. The phrases can be written on index cards for the students to choose from and use to formulate their suggestions. • I would like to suggest that _____ because _____. • I think that _____ might work well because _____. • Maybe we should think about _____ because _____. Pose problem-solving situations frequently so students can practice their suggestion-making skills.

Individual Objective	Strategy or Intervention
8. The student will not distract other students who are working.	Provide several alternatives for a student to work independently. Depending on the student's needs, she may be allowed to work with a buddy, sit at a table alone instead of a desk, work in a study carrel, or take her work to a quieter place like the library. As long as she works without distracting others, the student should be allowed to make the choice. Otherwise, restrict the student's choice until she earns the privilege by displaying responsible, respectful behavior.
9. The student will respect classmates' private time and/or private property.	Provide private areas in the room where students know they won't be interrupted. An area might be created behind a movable partition or in a study carrel. Establish a rule for the classroom that says a student is not to be bothered when she is in one of these areas. Before every work time, establish concrete guidelines for students to follow for respecting private time. For example, if students are assigned to read quietly, give them an exact time during which they are to remain quietly reading and what kind of behavior is expected during that time. If possible, also provide areas where students can safely place items they want kept private from others. Bins, covered boxes, and shelving may work as private storage areas accessible only by teacher permission.

Individual Objective	Strategy or Intervention
10. The student will respect teachers' private time.	As a teacher, let students know when it is okay to interrupt you. For example, if you plan to work at your desk as students are reading, you might ask students to get any questions or requests from you taken care of first. Then tell students they are to remain quiet and working until you are done at your desk and signal for them to stop. Be consistent in your requests and guidelines.
11. The student will offer a reasonable refusal when asked to share.	Make sure students know that they do have a right not to share on occasion. However, they need to handle the refusal in a kind manner. Teach them to say things in a neutral manner like "I'd rather not share my _____ right now" or "Not today, but another day I might."

▶ Respect for Property

1. The student will recognize her own property.	Purchase a label-making machine or devise another labeling system and make sure each student's possessions are labeled with their first and last names. Provide a box, a "cubby," or a desk for the students to put their items in so each day they can keep materials organized and protected. When students bring in items from home for temporary use, make sure those items have also been labeled prior to being brought in.

Individual Objective	**Strategy or Intervention**
2. The student will take good care of her own belongings.	Build in time to your daily routine for students to organize and put away belongings. This can be hanging up coats and getting materials out of desks or lockers or organizing backpacks to take home for the night. As students organize, praise them and provide care tips. For students who may have less, arrange to have extra belongings on hand for them to use and care for including backpacks, stuffed animals, toys, games, pleasure reading books, school materials, outerwear, and so on. Businesses often partner with schools and may be willing to provide these items for care and use.
3. The student will ask permission to use the teacher's property.	Create a sign-out sheet to record any item a student borrows from you to ensure its return. The sign-out sheet can also document who had an item in case it fails to be treated properly. Put the sign-out sheet on a clipboard in an easy-to-locate area like your desk or where materials like books, paper, and pencils are typically stored. Have fun with how you title the sheet (e.g., "Be sure to sign the sheet when you take things from my warehouse!"), but be totally serious about expecting items to be treated well and returned in a timely manner.

Ms. Brown's Materials Sign-Out Sheet

Student's Name	Date	Item Borrowed	Condition When Returned

(reproducible full-size copy on page 164)

Individual Objective	Strategy or Intervention
4. The student will ask permission to use others' property.	Teach students to ask permission to use other people's property whether it belongs to the teacher or to a student. Role-play different ways students might ask permission. Be sure to stress the importance of asking first and not taking the item until permission has been granted. Expect students to ask whether it's something as small as a pencil or as large as a basketball. By using the sign-out sheet in Individual Objective #3 on the previous page, and establishing asking permission as a general practice in your classroom, you create an environment of respect for individual and classroom property. Be sure to allow a couple of minutes at the end of each class for items to be returned to their proper owners and proper places.
5. The student will be able to use and return other's property in good condition.	Until you know how well a student treats property, whether it's hers, the school's, or someone else's, require her to seek permission from you before asking to borrow from someone else. When an item is to be returned, she should show you its condition and then return the item to the owner.

Improving Self-Esteem

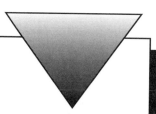

> Profane language flies rampantly in the hallway outside the high school "BD Room." Sullen looks, disrespectful behavior, lack of cooperation—the stereotypical descriptors of students with behavior problems—are perceived by other students and teachers passing by in the hallway. Such students and their behaviors are deemed "hopeless and incorrigible" by others, including the administration sometimes, and so they're often housed off the beaten path and away from the mainstream of school.

First of all, students with behavior disorders need to be surrounded by students with strong self-esteem who can act as good behavioral and psychological role models. Hopefully your students with behavior disorders are included in the regular classroom as much as possible to foster positive self-images and behavior. Secondly, it's important for your students' individual behavioral and psychological needs to be addressed. Though each student may be diagnosed as having a behavior disorder that interferes with conduct and learning, each one has unique needs.

When students' individual psychological needs are addressed, they can learn how to present and be their best selves. Students can achieve genuine self-esteem, self-respect, and self-acceptance by growing in the following areas:

- taking responsibility for actions and moods
- recognizing strengths and weaknesses
- advocating for own needs
- sharing feelings and opinions
- learning how to present a healthy, positive self-image
- treating others well

The objectives, strategies, and interventions in this chapter will help your students learn how to "put the best foot forward," gaining self-respect and the respect of others in the process.

Yearly Goal: to develop positive self-esteem and self-acceptance

Individual Objective	Strategy or Intervention
1. The student will be able to recognize his own feelings and moods.	Help students develop a vocabulary for expressing their moods and feelings. Frequently address moods and feelings related to activities you do. For example, if you're reading a story, you might say something like "If that happened to me, I would be angry and annoyed" and elicit student responses to the same story or situation. If a student has done a task well, ask questions to emphasize emotions like "Aren't you proud of yourself for that?"
2. The student will be able to recognize the degree of his own emotions. 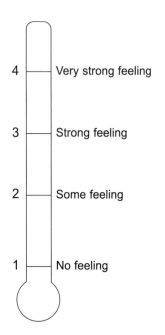 (reproducible full-size copy on page 165)	Frequently students may feel excessive anger or frustration about relatively minor situations or annoyances. Help students gain a more realistic perspective by comparing the situation to something that actually may be more serious. Provide an example, like getting to school tardy, and then say, "What would you rate this situation on the 'Feel-o-Meter' (or 'Feeling Rater')?" (Use the worksheet on page 165.) Follow up with a comment like "What might have a higher rating?" Then problem solve the situation together so the student can adjust his degree of emotion to a more appropriate level.

Individual Objective	Strategy or Intervention
3. The student will recognize and respond appropriately to the moods of others.	Pay more attention to good, productive, helpful moods than to negative moods of your students. Make it a habit to compliment, relax, and have fun with students. For students with pervasively negative moods, provide a comforting area where you can isolate them temporarily or they can isolate themselves until they're ready to deal more positively with others. For a student who is being overly critical, bossy, or whiny, you can say, "When you choose to be helpful and kind, we'd love to have you join us." Be consistent in what you say and do each time.
4. The student will be aware of causes and changes in his own emotions.	Students with behavior disorders or emotional problems can benefit from daily journaling to get in touch with and deal with their feelings. Pick a regular time each day for students to write quietly for ten minutes or so. Put on some quiet music and write along with the students. To help engage students in the journaling process, you may want to set up a consistent framework of questions like those on the left. Let students know, however, that they can write about whatever they wish. Unless students volunteer to share what they've written, let them know that you will not read what they write and it's to be kept private.

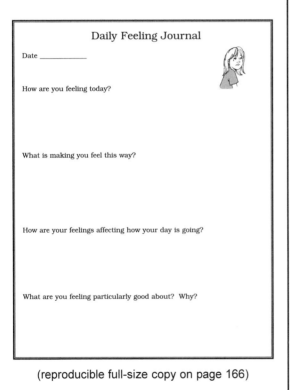

Daily Feeling Journal

Date _____

How are you feeling today?

What is making you feel this way?

How are your feelings affecting how your day is going?

What are you feeling particularly good about? Why?

(reproducible full-size copy on page 166)

Individual Objective	Strategy or Intervention
5. The student will take responsibility for his own actions and not blame others.	Confront students privately about any infractions so they don't feel the need to save face by projecting blame on others. Be specific in what you observed the student do and what you expect for appropriate behavior the next time. Avoid providing consequences initially so your discussion with the student is more for problem-solving and eliciting cooperation. Involve outside resources only when infractions are chronic and it is clear that the student needs more help developing inner control.
6. The student will attempt new activities, responsibilities, and assignments.	Refrain from grading or evaluating anything the student tries for the first time. For an assignment, you can simply put a check mark in your grade book to show the student did what he was asked. For activities or responsibilities, have the student reflect on how he did. If needed, discuss ways to improve the next time.
7. The student will praise and compliment others.	Have students role-play with partners how to tell someone what they like. Students can create their own situations and decide what to say. Let partners share with the class, coaching students if their praise needs to be more sincere and positive.

Individual Objective	Strategy or Intervention
8. The student will respond appropriately to praise and compliments.	Create a positive, accepting and tolerant classroom environment by making praise and compliments an everyday occurrence in your classroom rather than criticisms and confrontations. At the end of each class or student session, sincerely compliment specific students and/or the class on what went well. Point out any individual progress, kind acts by others, and particularly instances where students worked or interacted well together. Or at the end of each day, have students reflect in journals and then discuss what deserves to be praised that day. Students can even praise school lunch if they want.
9. The student will take appropriate care of his own personal appearance.	Some students may not know how to take care of their personal hygiene, or they may not have the facilities at home or the parental guidance to ensure that they take care of themselves. If needed, arrange for a private showering or clean-up place and time for a student, particularly if that student is picked on for his appearance. Arrange to have appropriate clothes available that have been donated or perhaps even purchased by the school.

Elicit the help of a PE teacher, the school nurse, a guidance counselor, or the school psychologist if you feel it's in the student's best interest for you not to be directly involved. |

Individual Objective	Strategy or Intervention
10. The student will identify his own personal qualities.	Frequently have students make class projects related to the curriculum that allow them to share and talk about their own personal qualities. For example, if you're talking about heredity in science class, students could make a family tree of immediate family members and include some of their physical traits like hair color, eye color, and height, along with their names. Or if you read a story or book about a hero or heroine, students can then make a poster about themselves describing times they were heroic. Let students share their posters and projects if they want.
11. The student will identify his own strengths and weaknesses.	Many scholastic magazines and trade publications have questionnaires and inventories that accompany their articles. Whenever possible, let students complete and discuss such questionnaires. Older students can benefit from things like learning styles inventories, personality type questionnaires, and career interest inventories available commercially in print or online. Have students keep a portfolio of their inventories to look through as they learn more about their strengths, weaknesses, and interests and apply them to real life.
12. The student will attempt to handle problem situations.	Let students handle their own problems as much as possible. When intervention is needed, ask the student questions like those below to guide his thinking but do not solve the problem for him. Intervene only when the student tries to solve the problem in a way that will make the situation worse. 1. What exactly is the problem? 2. What choices do you have for solving it? 3. What do you think is the best choice? Why?

Individual Objective	Strategy or Intervention
13. The student will apply positive conflict resolution techniques.	Teach students a step-by-step method for positive conflict resolution. Using the worksheet on page 167, have students write at least one statement in answer to each question as part of their planning. Encourage the students to apply the steps on their own if possible.

Handle Conflicts Positively

Conflicts don't just disappear. You need to handle them positively in order to make the best of the situation. Fill in the steps below to help you through the conflict resolution process.

1. What is the conflict or problem?

2. Who or what do you have a conflict with? Why?

3. What do you want to happen instead?

4. What can you say or do to request what you want?

5. In what way should you say or do it?

6. Where should you say or do it?

(reproducible full-size copy on page 167)

If a student wants your help, have him make an appointment with you to sit in on a conflict resolution meeting with the involved individual. Let the student know that you are there for moral support and will intervene only if he requests it.

14. The student will share constructive feelings about a situation or activity.	Elicit feedback from students frequently about what they like or have learned from a lesson or situation. Use the feedback and comments to plan future activities. Coach students to make suggestions rather than complain or put down a situation or activity. Listen and incorporate their suggestions as much as possible so they know that their feelings and input count.

Individual Objective	Strategy or Intervention
	If you sense that a student is hesitant to share feelings or make suggestions, encourage him to share them privately with you. Frequently ask your students, "What did you think about that?" or "How did you like that?" or "How did that go for you?" so your classroom becomes a community of learners who share and learn from each other.
15. The student will make positive comments about himself. 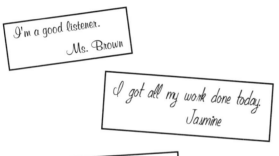	Create a bulletin board for students to write and post positive comments about themselves on a regular basis (e.g., daily or at least weekly). Encourage students to add comments whenever they feel like it, and have them sign their comments so they can take credit. Be sure to add your own comments about yourself too. Positive comments can range from praise of themselves to sharing something they enjoyed. Sharing and posting positive comments is likely to foster more positive conversation in your classroom as students look and stand around the bulletin board, so be sure to allow time for it.
16. The student will use appropriate body language to show interest and motivation.	Insist that students use body language in class to show that they are being attentive (even if perhaps they are not) and care about how they appear to others. Expect students to sit upright and look forward. When another student is speaking, students should be attending to the teacher or the student, depending on which one is in their line of vision. When outside speakers are present in the room, students should be expected to have the same attentive, caring appearance.

Individual Objective	Strategy or Intervention
17. The student will develop a realistic and positive attitude about experiences.	Before a student undertakes an activity, task, or new experience, discuss what's to be expected in terms of behavior, feelings, and results. Talk about what typically happens from your point of view and also what you've observed to be experienced by other students. Tailor your comments to the student's needs, interests, and abilities.
18. The student will be able to accept that everyone makes mistakes.	As long as a student is willing to make repeated attempts at success with a task or activity, allow him to keep working at it. Encourage the student to work out a reasonable time line with you that allows him time to improve. As much as possible, "grade" students on expanding the amount and kinds of things they try or areas they explore (gaining experience) rather than being right or wrong. Frequently provide activities and experiences just for the purpose of doing and having them as means of exploration and interest and not for their concrete outcomes.
19. The student will identify self put-downs and their effects.	Self put-downs can be a sign of frustration or means of avoiding something. With the student, decide when he tends to put himself down. Is it during certain activities that are more difficult or is it with other students with whom he's less comfortable? Problem solve together how to handle the frustrations so he feels better about himself or how to handle the situation successfully rather than avoiding it.

Individual Objective	Strategy or Intervention
20. The student will understand and accept the value in sharing and discussing problems with others.	Hold small group problem-solving sessions on a regular basis. Keep groups no larger than three or four students. Initially pose problems for the students to solve that are typical for students their age. Have the students come up with several alternatives for each problem. As the group bonds and becomes comfortable with one another, encourage students to suggest other problems for the group to talk about. If a student requests confidence (i.e., keeping the information secret) from group members, ensure that the group agrees before the problem is discussed.
21. The student will use a confident voice.	Every day when students enter your room, greet them at the door with a confident voice and a hand shake so they get used to direct, personal interaction with an adult. Then, in class, insist that students talk in a voice that's loud enough and confident enough to be heard by everyone so they get used to projecting their voices with the intent to be heard and paid attention to.
22. The student will have patient expectations of himself.	As much as possible, set goals for students and help students set goals for themselves that promote individual progress and not comparisons to other students. For example, in a math class, rather than "grading" everything the student does against a class answer key, grade the student based on how much better he did than last time or how many math skills or objectives he has mastered in comparison to what he knew before. For an older student, successfully doing a short stint of volunteer work may be just as significant as landing that first job.

Reassure students that they are doing their best to meet goals. Praise efforts like attempting new activities, improving work skills, or learning new skills rather than giving scores, grades, or prizes. |

Individual Objective	Strategy or Intervention
23. The student will be comfortable taking personal risks to contribute in class and during social conversations and interactions.	Be sure to set a classroom tone and climate that ensures respect is shown among your students and to you. Make sure students adhere consistently to turn-taking rules so every student can be heard. Provide plenty of wait time during discussions and conversations so students have equal opportunity to think through what they want to say. Also ban any put-downs or criticisms of another's comments or suggestions. Build in free time when students can have relaxed conversations with each other and get practice in the give-and-take of listening and conversing.
24. The student will be punctual.  You have a 4:00 appointment for an interview at the grocery store. The store is a 15-minute drive from your home. When should you plan to leave home to get there? The school bus arrives to pick you up at 8:15. It's a 5-minute walk to the bus stop. What time should you start gathering your things to go out the door?	First of all, make sure the student has a watch of his own so he has no excuse for not knowing the time. Also make sure the time is accurately set and that the student can tell time. If he has difficulty telling time, encourage the use of a digital watch. Then rehearse scenarios like the ones on the left where the student has to plan how to be on time. Be sure to discuss other things to consider like having reliable transportation to help in getting places on time, the need to include time for gathering belongings, and the value of arriving at an appointment or destination early.
25. The student will be able to be trusted on errands.	Initially have the student do the same errand each time. For example, the student might take the milk order for snack time to the cafeteria to the same person and at the same time each day. If needed, the student can take a pass or sign-off sheet to be signed upon the student's arrival with the time. As the student increases his trustworthiness, have him try other kinds of errands with more flexibility in time and place.

Individual Objective	Strategy or Intervention
26. The student will take good care of possessions.	Students need to understand that part of how others develop trust in someone is determined by how they take care of things and the general impression they make of conscientiousness and caring. Discuss how people make judgments about whether to loan someone something based on their impression of how that person takes care of his own possessions. If a student borrows things and returns them in poor shape, refrain from allowing the student to borrow again until the student proves himself. Also encourage parents not to replace possessions students mistreat so they face the natural consequences of their actions.

If students leave books and notebooks and other things in the classroom or elsewhere, take the items and put them away somewhere. When the student discovers they're missing, let the student know where they are and that they can be returned if he promises to keep track of them. If needed, come up with more significant consequences for students who repeatedly fail to take care of their materials and possessions. |
| 27. The student will care about the personal impression or image he presents. | Provide grooming and toiletry items in your room for students who may need encouragement in taking care of their personal appearance. Initially let students know where those items are in case they want to use them on their own. Have enough so students don't need to share any items. Also have a mirror in the room for students to check out their appearances. If needed, talk with any students who need to take better care of themselves. |

Individual Objective	Strategy or Intervention
	For older students, you can have lessons on the impact of personal image on getting a job, gaining admittance to college, and winning over a member of the opposite sex. Older students may also benefit from being taught to do their own laundry so they can maintain an appropriate appearance. If your school has laundry facilities, take your students there and teach them clothing care skills. With older students, also discuss the impression they make with their ability to appear organized, as well as having good hygiene and a confident presence. For example, taking an organizer or appointment book and pen along to an interview may show a potential employer that you pay attention to needed details and information.
28. The student will be able to assess and negotiate how to meet his own needs.	A good place for students to apply negotiating skills and the communication needed for it to happen is within the classroom and the school setting. Let students know that you are open to adjusting things like assignment expectations, homework due dates, and choice of activities provided that the request and reasoning is sound. For example, if the class suggests an alternate activity to one you suggest, discuss it, and as long as it meets the same objective, do the activity. Or if a student finds an assignment more difficult than expected, encourage him to negotiate with his teacher for more help and more time. Stress how most needs can be met through negotiation as long as ideas are expressed clearly and respectfully.

Individual Objective	Strategy or Intervention
29. The student will recognize when to compromise.	Teach students the concept of win-win compromising through frequent role-playing. Present a situation and have students role-play from three different perspectives: one person winning and one losing, vice versa, and both people winning. Follow up with a discussion on how compromise happens. Be sure to provide example situations from home, school, interacting with friends, and work as appropriate.

Planning a Win-Win Compromise

Situation: Jeremy has been asked to go to the football game Saturday night and for pizza afterward with his friends. He usually has a 10:00 curfew but needs a later one so he can enjoy both activities with his friends.

Name who might win or lose in each section below. Then describe the possible outcomes.

Win-Lose: Parents   win.
              Jeremy   loses.
Jeremy's parents tell him he cannot go because the activities go past his curfew time and his curfew never changes.

Lose-Win: Jeremy   wins.
              Parents   lose.
Jeremy's parents give in to his request though they are not comfortable with the situation.

Win-Win: Jeremy   and
              his parents   both win.
Jeremy's parents agree to the later curfew as long as Jeremy calls them at 10:00 and tells them where he is and when he thinks he will be home.

(reproducible full-size copy on page 168)

30. The student will be able to accept and recover from disappointment.	Students generally feel true disappointment when something they really wanted to have or to have happen does not. Students can best prepare for disappointment by keeping their expectations realistic. Have students anticipate possible outcomes before something happens, both positive and negative, and how they might handle each. If disappointment occurs, have students reflect on the occurrence for next time. They can ask themselves, "How can I improve next time?" or "How can I get or do what I want next time?"

Individual Objective	Strategy or Intervention
31. The student will express active interest with appropriate smiling and nodding.	Frequently sit down across from students and actively listen to them during discussion or conversation rather than "overseeing" and monitoring them. Practice the same active listening skills, posture, eye contact, and facial expressions you expect them to give back to you and to others. Have another teacher, assistant, or adult in the room free you from distraction so you can pay undivided attention. Invite other adults into the classroom from time to time just to sit and engage your students in face-to-face, active conversation.
32. The student will be able to recognize the effect of decisions on himself and others.	Provide the student with a consistent framework to use when considering what decisions to make so he can predict results. Work through a few examples with the student from time to time so he can internalize the process and use it regularly.

Thinking Through a Decision

My Decision

Meet with friends instead of working on my project.

Effects on Me

Effects on Others

Have fun, fail the project.

Let down my group members. Group members get a failing grade.

(reproducible full-size copy on page 169)

Improving Self-Control

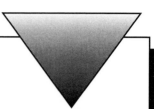

It's Monday morning and Jim sits outside the door of his first period class. Almost half an hour remains before class starts, but Jim is too tired or perhaps too depressed to seek out friends like his high-school peers do after a weekend.

Jim has spent the weekend with his dad and stepmother, both of whom over-control Jim's behavior through isolation and loss of privileges and constantly compare him to a seemingly more perfect younger brother (information gleaned during many IEP meetings, counseling sessions, and Jim's self report).

Granted, Jim does have behavioral difficulties due to his attention deficit disorder. On a good day, Jim may be silly, immature, and inattentive, but he still remains upbeat and tries to do class work. On his worst days, he constantly berates himself saying "You know I'm stupid" or "I can't do that" and chooses instead to put down his head and withdraw. However, Jim is never malicious, mean, defiant, or disrespectful.

Because of over-control and perhaps excessive behavioral management in the past, Jim basically has no recognition of himself. He sees in himself only what is reflected by the significant adults in his life and other students around him.

Jim's case is an extreme example, to be sure, but it is illustrative of what can happen when a student is over-managed and does not learn self-control and self-management of behavior.

As teachers, it is important that we provide ways for students to have power, competence, and choice in their lives and to learn to regulate their own behaviors. They will need to do so in their adult lives. You can help students develop self-control and responsible behavior by helping them grow in the following areas:

- expressing feelings
- developing appropriate behavior
- considering impact of their behavior on others
- accepting consequences
- exhibiting ethical behaviors
- having positive self-respect
- developing a positive attitude

The objectives, strategies, and interventions in this chapter will help your students learn responsible behavior and self-control.

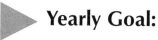 **Yearly Goal:** to develop control over own behaviors

Individual Objective	Strategy or Intervention
1. The student will adjust to a change in routine. **News for Tomorrow** Awards Assembly at 11:00 Class Schedule Reading 9:00—10:00 Math 10:00—11:00 Awards Assembly 11:00—11:45 Regular Schedule after assembly	Most of us adapt to changes more appropriately if we are prepared for them. At a regular time each day, prepare your students for any changes in routine that will occur the next day. You might want to give the time a name like *News for Tomorrow* or *Tomorrow's Agenda*. Changes announced during that time might include schedule rearrangements for assemblies, having a substitute teacher, early dismissal for teacher meetings, practice fire drills, and so on. Allow plenty of time for students to ask questions so they understand how the changes affect them. Post the changes on the chalkboard as a reminder for the next day. Be sure to talk privately with any individual students who may need more reassurance about the changes or who have other personal changes in routine, like having to leave early for an appointment or needing to miss part of a class to meet with the school psychologist.
2. The student will adapt behavior so it's appropriate to the situation. *Partner Work* Use quiet conversational voices. Each person participates. Stay on task. *Nature Center Visit* Be quiet and listen. Raise hand for questions. Remember to ask to touch something. *Fire Drill* Line up at the door. Walk quietly and quickly down the stairs. Go to the school sign in front of the building. Stand quietly with the class.	All students need reminders about expected behavior in given situations. Before students enter a new or different situation, discuss the behaviors expected. Even if students have been in the situation before, don't assume they remember. Role-play and/or list behaviors on the chalkboard to help students understand. Don't hesitate to cover everything the student needs to do to meet your expectations. On the other hand, don't belabor or over-explain your expectations with the anticipation that students won't behave well. Simply state your expectations in a positive manner that suggests you expect them to be able to exhibit the appropriate behavior.

Individual Objective	Strategy or Intervention
3. The student will exhibit self-control.	For a student to learn self-control, she needs to know what it looks like in each situation she enters. Give the student very concrete guidelines for self-control and review them each time the student enters a particular situation. In your classroom, you might expect the student to stay seated, keep her hands off others, and raise her hand for questions or attention instead of blurting out comments. Enlist the support of the student's other teachers to help set concrete parameters for self-control. For example, the PE teacher may allow running and free play, but the student must limit where she runs and keep her hands off others.
4. The student will refrain from making inappropriate comments.	First keep an anecdotal record and tally for a few days when and where the student is making inappropriate comments. You may also want to note the kinds of things she's saying and to whom. Be sure to make the observations in several settings and enlist the student's other teachers as needed. Review the record to see if there's a pattern for where, when, to whom, or under what circumstances the student makes inappropriate comments. Some students may not understand what's inappropriate to say and will need direct instruction, while other students may be taking frustrations or anxieties out on others. Talk with the student about what you observe and problem solve together how to decrease inappropriate comments.

Record of Inappropriate Comments

Name Aron S.   Teacher Mr. Grove

Date Nov. 14

Situation or Class _____ Reading _____

Frequency	When	What Kind of Comment	To Whom
/ / /	during reading group	criticizes other students' reading attempts	Natasha, Johnna, Richard

(reproducible full-size copy on page 170)

Individual Objective	Strategy or Intervention
5. The student will display the appropriate level of energy or excitement for a situation.	For students with excess energy and/or problems with attention, make sure they have plenty of transition time for a new situation. First of all, if they need to tone down their energy level for the situation, make sure they've had a recess or "body break" of some kind to rid themselves of extra energy. Then have them return to the room and sit quietly for a few minutes before entering the new situation. If students will be entering a situation where excitement, noise, and laughter is expected, be sure they know what level of energy is appropriate. Be very clear with expected behaviors by providing examples (e.g., okay to stand, to clap, to talk).
6. The student will be honest in behavior and words.	Remove the temptations and frustrations that can cause a student to cover up the truth through words or actions. Avoid leaving a student in a room alone where she may be tempted to take others' belongings. Make sure work and expectations are reasonable for the student so she doesn't feel that she needs to lie to cover up any anger or frustration.
7. The student will maintain an appropriate voice tone and volume level.	Coach the student on the appropriate tone and volume to use in various situations. Before each situation, let the student know what's expected. For example, during partner work time, you might allow students to talk softly between themselves as they work. In the hallway, students might either be expected to be silent or to talk softly. If a student becomes angry or overly excited, talk to her in a soft voice to calm her and help her regain control of her voice and volume.

Individual Objective	Strategy or Intervention
8. The student will use appropriate language in the classroom and hallways.	When students become part of your classroom, let them know exactly what kind of language is expected. If it's at the beginning of the year, have a class meeting and let them know that profanity is not tolerated in the classroom and that how you talk is how you show respect for yourself and for others. As other students enter throughout the year, let them know what you consider unacceptable language. There needs to be immediate consequences for infractions related to profanity, as that is one area that should be non-negotiable. Most schools have clear rules regarding it.
9. The student will respect the school's property.	Use specific examples to describe how you want students to take care of school property, whether it's the top of their desks or picking up litter from the floor and putting it in the trash. Praise and thank students for caring for their areas. If there are problems, have the individual student take steps at a later, private time to remedy the situation. For example, the student can wash her desk off after school or erase pen/pencil marks from a book.
10. The student will respect others' property.	Set rules in your classroom for students to use another person's property. Whether a student is borrowing a pencil from you or paper from another student, the student should ask politely to borrow the item before taking it and express thanks when she returns it. Expect students to repair or replace another's property if they fail to ask permission and then damage it in any way.

Individual Objective	Strategy or Intervention
11. The student will develop appropriate ways to handle stress and nervousness.	Having and understanding enough information about a situation helps a student handle it more appropriately. Symptoms like crying, whining, or perseverating on a topic indicate that a student has misconceptions or is lacking information about something new. Before new situations, tasks, or activities, prepare the student as much as possible and allow her to ask questions. Be sure the student knows who she might talk to later on if she has more questions or concerns.
12. The student will learn that one's behavior is a choice.	When requesting cooperation or involvement from a student, provide her with options to choose from. For example, she might choose to work with the partner you've assigned or work quietly alone at a study carrel. On the playground, the student can be given the choice of following the rules for a game or playing by herself on playground equipment. Enlist the help of the student's other teachers in providing the student with options and corresponding behavior to choose from.
13. The student will recognize the causes and effects of behaviors.	Use the student's behavior (positive and negative) as experiences to be learned from. When something good happens, ask the student why it occurred. Have her reflect on which behaviors and choices led to the positive outcome. When an experience is negative and the corresponding behavior inappropriate, ask the student what she has learned and what she'd do differently next time.

Individual Objective	Strategy or Intervention
14. The student will recognize her degree of personal control over events.	As much as possible, provide the student with opportunities for planning and decision making. Encourage parents and other significant adults to allow the student such opportunities. The student can be given responsibilities ranging from getting up and getting to school on time to arranging and preparing for a job interview. Whatever the experience and its outcome, the student will learn from making her own decisions and anticipating events.
15. The student will gauge the intensity of her feelings.	Provide a rating scale for the student to use to measure her level of anger. For example, if you use a 1 to 5 rating scale (with 5 being the highest), the student can say, "I'm so mad. I'm at a 4." Younger or less verbal students can hold up fingers to show the appropriate level. Students who can rate their feelings might be less likely to use profanity or other inappropriate means to express the intensity of their anger or other feeling. Coach students in ways to handle their feelings if they register 3 or higher.
16. The student will use self-talk for emotional control.	Encourage students to have inner dialogues to help sort out their feelings. In a quiet spot, guide a student through questions like the following to help her carry on an inner dialogue. 1. What would you say to someone else if this happened to them? 2. How could they make it better? 3. Now talk to yourself the same way you would talk to that person about it.

Individual Objective	Strategy or Intervention
	After a few sessions, the student can hopefully use self-talk independently. For students who can write, it may be more comfortable for them to journal their thoughts as a means of inner dialogue. You could have already prepared sheets with the questions above to guide their thinking. If students want, they can share what they write with you for feedback or reassurance.
17. The student will manage her own anger.	Provide a place where a student can calm down when she's becoming angry or frustrated. Make an agreement ahead of time about how she'll signal you and where she'll go. She might say, "I need to go in the hallway for a minute" where you'll expect her to stand quietly, think the situation over, and then reenter the classroom when she's calm. Let the student know you're available to talk with her if she requests, but do so when it doesn't interrupt what other students are doing.
	Be clear with the student about what is not acceptable for handling anger, like punching someone else, swearing, or throwing her materials down. Those types of disruptive and potentially threatening behaviors require that you send the student out of the classroom.
18. The student will assess consequences of her own behavior with regard to her own best interests.	When you have enough anecdotal information to see a pattern of behavior emerging, meet with the student to talk about it. Share your observations. Ask the student what she's feeling when the behavior occurs and what she thinks causes it. Discuss what she can do differently to have things happen that promote her needs and best interests instead of interfering with them.

Improving Self-Control
The Behavior Disorder IEP Companion

115

Individual Objective	Strategy or Intervention
19. The student will recognize the results of acting impulsively.	The student exhibiting impulsivity needs direct instruction in and reminders about using "thinking behavior." Come up with a short phrase you can use to cue the student to think before acting. Make an agreement with the student that you will help her think before acting so she has better results for her actions (keep the focus positive.) You can say something like "Jessie, stop and think" or simply the word "Think" coupled with a direct gaze at the student. Choose a phrase that you can use in the middle of class activities or discussion.

Stop to Think

1. What will I say?

2. What will I do?

3. What might happen because of what I do or say?

4. Should I do it? Why?

(reproducible full-size copy on page 171)

You can also use the phrase to prompt the student to write a plan before taking long-term action. For example, a student who decides she needs to physically confront a student after school can be sent to a private space to write out her plan and hopefully draw a better conclusion.

Individual Objective	Strategy or Intervention
20. The student will lessen or eliminate demanding behavior.	First try ignoring the demanding behavior to see if the student can resort to more appropriate behavior to meet her needs. You will need to consistently ignore such behavior each time for the student to get the message that appropriate, not demanding, behavior gets the attention she wants. If planned ignoring doesn't work and it appears the student may not have the skill, stop the student and provide her with the language to make an appropriate request. She can learn to ask questions accompanied by the word "please" or to say things like "I'd like to _____, please." Reward any approximations of appropriate requests as she gets closer to the desired behavior.

Individual Objective	Strategy or Intervention
21. The student will postpone and think over behavior related to a negative emotion.	Set an example for your students by delaying action as a result of any anger, frustration, or disappointment you feel about a situation. Frequently say to your students, "I need time to think about that before I do anything (or talk about it). It's important to think this over well."
22. The student will make a decision without peer pressure.	When asking for student input or "votes" on something, have students respond in writing on paper or ballots rather than raising their hands. With more private means of sharing, students are less likely to be influenced by their peers and feel that their own voices count.
23. The student will be patient when dealing with problems. **Situation:** Before I go to lunch, I have to drop my books off at my locker. By the time I get my lunch, all the seats are taken at the table where my friends sit and I have to sit alone or with kids I don't know. **Alternative 1:** Ask one of my friends to save me a seat at the table. **Alternative 2:** Ask one of my friends to sit with me at the other table so I know at least one person there and can get comfortable getting to know the others.	When meeting with a student to problem solve a situation, have her come up with one solution and two alternative solutions. Have the student anticipate what will happen as a result of the first solution. Reassure the student that some problems take more work to solve than others. Together talk about when the student might need to try the other two solutions.

Individual Objective	Strategy or Intervention
24. The student will prioritize what and when to problem solve.	Have the student keep a problem-solving journal to write in regularly. Discuss how all people have to problem solve situations on a daily basis. Initially provide the student with sample situations for practice. Have the student rate the problem from 1 to 3 using the rating scale on the left. Then, as indicated, have the student suggest solutions. After some practice, have the student record her own situations, ratings, and attempts at problem solving.

Problem-Solving Journal

Rating Scale

1 A small problem. I can handle it on my own or perhaps even ignore it.

2 A medium-sized problem. I need to solve it soon and plan carefully what to do.

3 A big problem. I need help from someone else and may need other resources.

Problem-solving situation: I share a locker with Mike. Mike used my gym clothes because he forgot his. I have gym tomorrow and Mike hasn't returned my gym clothes.

Rating: 2

Solution: Ask Mike to return the gym clothes by tomorrow. Bring an extra set in case Mike forgets or is absent.

Problem-solving situation:

Rating:

Solution:

Problem-solving situation:

Rating:

Solution:

(reproducible full-size copy on page 172)

Individual Objective	Strategy or Intervention
25. The student will use goal setting to overcome failure.	Provide students with "second chances" whether it's a second chance related to an incident of inappropriate behavior (as long as it's not harmful to her or to others) or to a poorly done project or assignment. Have the student meet with you to problem solve what she'll do to either learn from her behavior or to improve upon her assignment. Have the student spell out what steps she'll take to improve upon the situation. Together discuss specific behavioral expectations and time lines for improvement or for completing a task. Then let the student try again. Meet later to discuss the results of the goal setting.

Individual Objective	Strategy or Intervention
26. The student will identify moods and handle moodiness appropriately.	When you notice a student is moody, have her journal write a response to statements like those on the left to help her recognize and explain what she's feeling. Raising the student's awareness about her own mood and how it is perceived by others is important to her being able to cope with changing moods in herself and others. Have the student respond to mood statements about positive moods, too, so she can compare effects of different moods on herself and others.

What's Your Mood?

Fill in the following statements.

1. I'm in a _____ mood.

2. I feel this way because _____
   _____
   _____
   _____

3. My mood might affect other people by _____
   _____
   _____
   _____

4. My mood will go away or get better once _____
   _____
   _____
   _____

(reproducible full-size copy on page 173)

Individual Objective	Strategy or Intervention
27. The student will cope with unreasonable fears related to new situations.	Take the student through a rehearsal of the situation to alleviate any fears. Describe where she'll go and what will happen step-by-step. If possible, visit the place where the new experience will occur. Have her meet any new people involved. Allow the student to ask questions to gain the information she needs to feel more confident about the situation.

Individual Objective	Strategy or Intervention
28. The student will learn techniques for dealing with worry, fear, and anxiety.	Provide a refuge within the classroom for students to go to if worry, fear, or anxiety is overwhelming them. You might provide a quiet area with a beanbag chair to sit in, paper, pencil, books, and a CD player with earphones. On a prearranged signal, allow the student to go to the quiet spot. Encourage the student to think through or write about what's bothering her as she relaxes. After 10 minutes or so, have the student return to the expected activity. If needed, she can signal to you that she needs to talk to you or to someone else when she's ready.
29. The student will identify and change intense negative feelings.	Students need to recognize negative feelings before they can change them. With the student, list negative feelings. After each feeling, make a list of how someone acts when they have this feeling. Discuss the common things in the list and how they negatively affect the person who has the feeling and others.

Let younger or less verbal students draw pictures and discuss them with you.

Anger	yell at others, throw things, hit, cry
Fear	refuse to do something, cry, hide, withdraw
Frustration	cry, shout, damage something
Sadness	cry, hide, withdraw, get angry	

Individual Objective	Strategy or Intervention
30. The student will recognize and deal with cop-out behaviors. Situation: The student is required to have a signed permission slip to go on a field trip. The student forgot to get the slip signed and it's still at home. Cop-Out Behavior: The student says she left the slip in her locker and asks permission to go get it. Having to look for the missing slip will delay the teacher's reaction and any other consequences for the student. Better Solution: Ask the teacher if you can call home to ask a parent to bring the slip to you at school. Or, if possible, have your parent give verbal permission over the phone.	As a class, role-play the difference between responsible handling of a situation and a "cop-out." Then create situations for student pairs to discuss and label as appropriate problem solving or "cop-out." Older students, in particular, can recognize the difference. After role-playing, have a discussion about the fact that most of the time they can work out a positive solution with someone.
31. The student will make and live by positive affirmations.	Being able to develop positive attitudes can help students have better daily experiences. Help each student develop her own personal "mantra" for a daily affirmation. Discuss times when she might need to use the affirmation to stay focused on the positive. Some teachers like to put positive statements to think about each day on the chalkboard. (Check the Psychology and Self-Help section, for example, of bigger bookstores for books of affirmations your students might like.) Share your own positive affirmations with the student as models for the student.
32. The student will take risks in order to make growth. New Things Tried sauerkraut at my Aunt Beth's house Went to the mall by myself with friend Sarah Learned to Rollerblade	Have the student list new things she's learned recently or new activities and adventures she's tried. Put the list in a folder for the student to keep. You might have the student give the list a name like "New Things." As the student learns and tries other new things, have her add to the list. Challenge her to build on to the list over the school year with things she tries in and out of school. Encourage the student from time to time by saying, "Let's see if you can add another thing to your 'New Things' list." Have the student compare the old list with the new list from time to time so she can feel proud of her growth and risk taking.

Individual Objective	Strategy or Intervention

33. The student will recognize her own self-defeating behaviors.

Self-Defeating Behaviors

Behavior	Reaction of Others	Better Choice
Whining	Irritated by you Make fun of you Avoid you and don't help	Try it before making any comment. Ask for help. Make a suggestion in a nice way.
Being Negative	Think you have a bad attitude Leave you out because you're hard to get along with	Give something a chance. Say something positively.
Procrastinating	Think you're lazy Think you don't care Think you can't do it Think you're undependable	Ask for help. Ask for more time. Suggest a different way. Tell what you've done and when you'll be finished.
Avoidance	Think you can't do it Think you're not responsible Think you can't be trusted	Ask for help. Work it out with the person. Be honest.

(reproducible full-size copy on page 174)

Develop a chart of self-defeating behaviors and put it on an individual sheet for the student or make it into a poster for the class to refer to. Explain that self-defeating behaviors are ways we act that get in the way of people liking us or in things going well for us. Provide examples of self-defeating behaviors, how others react to them, and more effective choices for behavior.

34. The student will recognize unrealistic goals.

When a student sets an unrealistic goal, gently guide her through the thinking to help her draw the same conclusion. Ask the student neutral, reflective questions (e.g., "How long do you think it will take to do that?" "What will it cost?" "What skills does someone need to do that?" "What things do you need to do first?"). Together set a more realistic goal and let the student use you as a sounding board or ask another appropriate individual for help.

Individual Objective	Strategy or Intervention

35. The student will set realistic goals.

Goal-Setting Form

Goal _____ Today's Date _____

Materials/Resources _____

_____

_____

Time Needed _____ Due Date _____

How Success Will Be Measured _____

_____

_____

(reproducible full-size copy on page 175)

Use goal setting frequently with your students so they begin to internalize the self-examination process involved. Students can set goals for things like an assignment, what they want to do during a class period, or what they want to do for a week. Provide a form like the one on the left to help students evolve a process. Students can elect to review their goals for feedback with you or another interested adult. They may want to keep a notebook or folder of their goals using the form so they can later assess what they've successfully accomplished over a period of time.

36. The student will use rehearsal strategies and imagery for problem solving.

1. Define the problem.
2. Decide how you feel.
3. Think who might help you or what you need.
4. Rehearse in your mind what you might do.
5. Do it.

Have the student prepare a strategy card to keep with her to help apply the steps of problem solving. Before she handles a problem, she should go through the steps mentally. She should also imagine what someone else involved in the situation might say and do and how she would respond.

37. The student will use relaxation strategies to handle stress.

Use relaxation strategies in your classroom on a regular basis, especially when you sense that a student or the class in general feels somewhat stressed or needs to be calmed. Strategies can include things like turning lights low and listening to calming music, going outside for exercise instead of tackling assignments, or having students journal write quietly to examine feelings and stresses on paper. Ask your students for their own ideas to reduce stress and increase relaxation.

Individual Objective	Strategy or Intervention
38. The student will determine right from wrong and exhibit ethical behavior.	Students who obviously have no sense of right or wrong are likely in need of ongoing individual counseling. With parent permission, arrange for the student to have regular counseling sessions with the school psychologist or another counseling provider. Suggest that the counselor provide you with techniques to use with the student to help her carry over what she's learning into the classroom and her social interactions.
39. The student will be able to tell a truth from a lie.	When you detect that a student is not telling the truth, arrange to have a private conversation with her. Ask her to tell you the truth about the situation. If she does, praise her for being honest. If she still does not tell the truth, avoid a confrontation about it. In the future, however, continue to have conversations with her to get at the truth when you suspect she's lying. Hopefully she will conclude that honesty is an ongoing expectation of her behavior.
40. The student will identify the consequences of wrongdoing.	Students need to understand that consequences are often not punishments. More often than not, consequences are natural results of the choices someone makes. With your students, make a chart of "wrong" behaviors and the usual consequences.

Behavior	Result
dishonesty	others won't share their thoughts; don't trust you
stealing	others refuse to share; don't trust you
lying	no one believes you when you do tell the truth
breaking something	others won't loan you things or share with you
telling a secret	others won't confide in you

Individual Objective	Strategy or Intervention
41. The student will accept the consequences of wrongdoing.	Use problem solving rather than consequences to help a student learn from her inappropriate behavior. When something wrong happens, have a private counseling or coaching session with the student. Discuss what happened and the student's motives for the behavior. Talk about what the student can do next time. Let the student know, however, that if the behavior worsens and the student doesn't willingly try to work out the problem, she will have a particular consequence to follow.
42. The student will answer honestly about wrongdoing.	Any time you need to discuss a wrongdoing with a student, do so in a private place well away from other students and preferably not during class. Approach the student in a non-confrontational manner to best elicit information. Ask the student what she knows about what happened and avoid making any accusations or judgments. Also ask her what should be done about the situation. Allow the student to suggest ways to problem solve the situation as well as suggest possible consequences. Put as much control and decision making in the hands of the student so she learns that she has control and responsibility, rightly or wrongly, over handling situations and how they turn out.
43. The student will avoid wrongdoing when pressured by peers.	Seat positive role models near more vulnerable or easily-influenced students so they can interact. Purposefully arrange partner or team activities so the student is with other students who exhibit appropriate behavior.

Developing Real-World Transition Skills

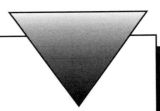

> Were you adequately equipped for the "real world" when you graduated from high school? Could you open a bank account, apply for a job, or make your own business or appointment phone calls easily? Probably not, but you probably had the social skills and critical thinking skills to help you interact with others to get and learn what you needed to survive.

Our students with behavior disorders find it tougher to make their way in the world today. Their impulsive decision making and inappropriate behaviors make it harder to get out of high school to begin with, and many of them have multiple brushes with school discipline policies and the law itself even before they're 18.

The middle school and high school years pass way too quickly for our students with behavior disorders. To better prepare such students, it is imperative that we begin transition work by age 14 and make it an integral component of their education every single day they attend school.

The individual objectives, strategies, and interventions in this chapter will help your students in the following areas:

- self-advocacy
- career exploration
- employability
- daily living skills
- communication

 **Yearly Goal:** to be prepared for future expectations and responsibilities

Individual Objective	Strategy or Intervention
1. The student will understand his rights as a student with behavioral needs.	Many students with behavior disorders receive extra support services through an Individual Education Plan (IEP) or a 504 Plan. Review a copy of the student's plan with him prior to beginning classes for the school year. Discuss what he's entitled to in his classes according to the plan as well as how the plan might affect disciplinary issues he may face. With increased awareness of his needs and rights, the student may be more likely to feel less frustrated as well as learn to advocate for his own needs.
2. The student will be actively involved in his IEP or 504 plan.	Prior to the student's annual IEP or 504 meeting, have him meet with his guidance counselor to review passing and graduation requirements. Together, they can assess how the student is doing and if he is meeting graduation expectations. Be sure to make counselors aware that some students with IEPs may have graduation requirements waived or substituted for or may be graduating based on IEP goals and objectives. They may be able to come up with a unique plan that meets individual and school requirements.

Individual Objective	Strategy or Intervention
3. The student will take an active part in monitoring his academic progress.	Have the student meet with his guidance counselor or academic advisor at least twice during the school year to review his current academic achievement. Together they can problem solve ways to help improve academic issues like attendance, completing work, or improving overall grades if necessary. Having a "neutral" staff member also involved in the student's education can provide a safe place for the student to voice frustrations and gain guidance and redirection.
4. The student will explore career and job skills as part of his educational plan.	From the time the student is a high school freshman, discuss the student's possible career plan and how academic courses fit in with it. The student's first two years are usually heavy with required courses, but there is usually some time to take courses for exploring career interests (e.g., welding, foods, auto mechanics). Encourage the student to take a couple of exploratory classes each school year to help fine tune long-range plans.
5. The student will help to create an appropriate academic plan.	When the student enters high school, arrange to have a meeting with the student, his guidance counselor, and the teacher who will oversee his academic and behavioral progress. Together, map out a four-year education plan, given his current career interests and his special academic and behavioral needs. The plan can then be reviewed and adjusted at the student's annual IEP meeting, as well as when scheduling classes for the next year. You may want to follow a year-by-year format like the one on the left.

Freshman Year Academic Plan

Required Classes	Classes for Career Exploration	Classes to Meet Individual Needs
English 9	Woodworking 1	Study Skills 1

(reproducible full-size copies on pages 176-177)

Individual Objective	Strategy or Intervention
6. The student will achieve maximum inclusion in the general education program.	As an adult, the student will deal with the mainstream of society or be "included" like any other person. While in school, have the student integrated in as many general education classes as possible. Arrange for appropriate behavioral and academic accommodations for the student with the general education teacher so the student can feel comfortable and successful. Providing appropriate behavioral models and challenging academic work may prove to be a good incentive for some students.
7. The student will problem solve any tardy or absenteeism problems.	To prepare a student for future employment and other scheduled responsibilities in the real world, he needs to learn to prevent tardy or absenteeism difficulties. Get the student's attendance report from the attendance office. Go over the report with the student to see if there are any patterns of tardiness or missed classes. If so, discuss their causes. Then, as needed, build punctuality into a positive incentive or grade/point earning system for the student. Problem solve together to target the classes or situations most affected. You may need to work something out with the main office so the student's attendance issues are dealt solely with the system you develop rather than being subjected to disciplinary consequences.

Individual Objective	Strategy or Intervention
8. The student will learn not to avoid responsibility.	Expect students to handle their responsibilities, whether it's something like completing an assignment or showing up on a job as part of work experience. Require that students do all of their assignments to pass rather than taking a zero and hoping to make it up with other assignments. If a student is employed, make a weekly check on his attendance and discuss any absences or tardies with him. If a student realizes that he's being held accountable through consistent monitoring and feedback, he may be more likely to follow through on assigned responsibilities. Be sure to provide positive feedback when the student handles responsibilities well.
9. The student will know where to look for a job.	Take your student on a job search field trip. Show the student where job information can be located, like in the school guidance office, on a bulletin board at a business, in a newspaper, and at a local employment office (like the state Workforce Center).
10. The student will be able to fill out a job application.	Obtain job applications from various employers and have students fill them out. Provide feedback to the student on his answers and the appearance of his application as if you were a potential employer. (Note: Applications can also be accessed online.)
11. The student will be able to interview for a job.	Practice interviewing skills with your students. Review the importance of proper dress, eye contact, a firm handshake, and presenting oneself confidently. Hold a mock interview before the student actually goes on a real one. Be sure to have the student generate and practice asking questions about benefits, company policies, and job duties.

Individual Objective	Strategy or Intervention
12. The student will be able to get a job.	Meet with the student immediately after he interviews for a job. Review how the interview went and then discuss what the student should do for follow-up, like write a thank-you note. Rehearse with the student how to make a follow-up call to check on his job status. Use a real phone so the simulation is as close to real as possible.
13. The student will be able to keep a job.	Once the student gets a job, enlist the help of a relevant staff member in monitoring the student's success on the job. The student can be enrolled in work experience as a credit and money-earning enterprise, be given a "job coach," or if the student would prefer, have you or someone else he respects check periodically with the employer to see how he's doing and provide feedback and job coaching.
14. The student will explore career and job opportunities.	The student's local community provides endless opportunities for exploring career and job interests. Schedule community speakers for your classes, college and technical school visits, industry tours, career fairs, and military recruiter visits as ways to periodically expose students to career and job opportunities.
15. The student will evaluate career skills and interests.	Arrange for the student to take career skill and interest inventories. Some inventories are provided via computer, like *Iowa Choices 2003**, and others can be obtained from military recruiting offices, community colleges, or local employment agencies. Encourage the student to evaluate his skills and interests through a variety of inventories.

* *Choices* is updated annually. It is available from the Iowa Center for Career and Occupational Resources (ICCOR), Iowa Department of Education, Grimes State Office Building, Des Moines, Iowa, 50319, 800-308-5993 (within Iowa), 515-242-5033 (outside Iowa) <http://www.state.ia.us/isoicc/is_choic.html>

Individual Objective	Strategy or Intervention
16. The student will choose a realistic future job or career.	Provide job shadowing experiences for the student so he knows what current job and career opportunities exist. Have the student list jobs or careers of potential interest. Each year the student is in school, provide a couple of job shadowing opportunities so he can continually evaluate his interests as well as his academic plans in relationship to possible future career plans.
17. The student will be able to handle conflict on the job. **Tips for Handling Conflicts at Work** • Supervisor—Complete the job as instructed. Then make an appointment to privately discuss the situation later with the supervisor in her office. • Customer—Enlist the help of another co-worker. Say, "I need to check with someone else about how to handle this." The break is a quick time-out for you and an opportunity to get a co-worker's help. • Co-worker—Don't get angry in front of the customers or your supervisor. Ask your co-worker if you can discuss the situation when you're on break. Express your viewpoint calmly. Listen to your co-worker's viewpoint.	Rehearse/role-play with the student ways to handle conflict with a supervisor, co-worker, and/or a customer. Prepare a tip sheet or index card like the one on the left to help remind the student.
18. The student will interact appropriately with supervisors and customers at work.	Work with the student to understand that instructions from supervisors and requests from customers are generally non-negotiable items. Have the student brainstorm ahead of time ways to lessen dissatisfaction with a task. For example, he may not like taking groceries to a customer's car, but it does get him exercise, fresh air, and possibly an opportunity to talk with someone he knows.

Individual Objective	Strategy or Intervention
19. The student will make small talk with customers and co-workers.	Give students opportunities to talk with a variety of people. Invite other school personnel into the classroom frequently to meet the students, like the librarian, the school psychologist, groundskeeper, or a favorite coach or lunch worker.
20. The student will ignore distractions so he can get a job done on time.	Just like on the job, provide specific time limits for students to complete a task in class for you, their school employer. For example, a reading assignment and accompanying questions may be due at 10:00. As long as a student is working without distraction, allow him to negotiate if more time is needed. However, consistently keep the same expectations so students become "trained" to be productive under given time lines.
21. The student will react appropriately to constructive criticism or suggestions.	Employers conduct employee evaluations, so you should conduct "student" evaluations to prepare the student for such reviews. For example, meet with the student twice a grading period to describe those behaviors that are successful and evaluate how they're affecting his grades and success. Also discuss any areas for improvement. Then set goals together. Prepare a written form ahead of time to reflect the evaluation and record goals. At the next evaluation, update the record and build on the student's performance.

Individual Objective	Strategy or Intervention
22. The student will learn to take the initiative in a situation.	Frequently let students make decisions and take leadership in class lessons, activities, and interactions. For example, you might assign a given project for an assignment but allow students to decide how the project is completed, or you may elicit students' opinions to help solve a situation in the classroom.
23. The student will work as a productive team member.	Put students together often to work on assignments and projects. Assign individual students to work together who have skills and personalities that complement one another. Also make situations real-life by occasionally putting together students who will need to negotiate differences in order to accomplish a task. From time to time, assign various roles to students, like Group Reporter, Group Note taker, or Group Leader, so they experience working with team members from a variety of perspectives.
24. The student will recognize and enlist the help of resources available after high school.	By a student's junior year, make sure he has met with your state vocational rehabilitation counselor and relevant members of other agencies to help with employment and daily living issues and needs. Oftentimes clients are placed on waiting lists so early application for services can be very beneficial.

Individual Objective	Strategy or Intervention
25. The student will earn his driver's license.	Many school districts no longer provide driver's education courses. However, if it is an IEP goal for a student to acquire his license for purposes of living independently and maintaining employment, then instructional and financial help may be available from a local education agency or vocational rehabilitation office. Work with the student and his parent(s) to arrange for driving lessons and financial help as needed.
26. The student will understand his rights and responsibilities as a citizen.	Obtain information for your older students on things like voter registration and voting, selective service registration, and tax laws. Review the materials with the student.
27. The student will contribute to his community.	Include community service and volunteering in the student's curriculum. Students may take on a project to read to younger students at a grade school, take care of lawns in the fall for the elderly, or clean up litter in a park as part of class work. A student might also earn school credit by providing a community service on a regular basis. For example, a student may help with an after-school program at a grade school and earn PE and/or work credit.

Individual Objective	Strategy or Intervention
28. The student will understand the consequences of illegal behavior.	Have a local police officer or your school resource officer speak to your students about illegal behaviors like harassment, physical assault, drug use and possession, and driving infractions. The officer should be very clear about when a student is considered an adult in the eyes of the law and possible consequences for illegal behaviors as an "adult." The officer should also offer to be a source of help for any students who are victims of illegal behavior.
29. The student will choose appropriate leisure-time activities.	Encourage students to become involved in clubs and activities to develop leadership and teamwork skills. If your students have an idea for a club, you may want to sponsor it. For example, they may wish to volunteer as mentors to younger students or organize an after-school basketball league for casual recreation.
30. The student will understand the concept and consequences of harassing behavior.	Invite a human resources director to talk to your students about different types of harassment, like verbal and sexual. Have the director discuss how the student should handle any harassment that occurs on the job as well as consequences if the student himself commits harassment. Follow up with a discussion of other types of harassment and how to handle them, like intrusion by a neighbor, or a former boyfriend who won't stop calling.

Individual Objective	Strategy or Intervention
31. The student will acquire real-life money and math skills.	Arrange for instruction for the student in the areas of checking, budgeting, paying bills, debit cards, credit cards, insurance, and car or transportation costs. The student can acquire skills through classes already offered at the school, like Consumer Math, Business Math, or Independent Living, or you might develop a unit using realistic materials to teach such skills.
32. The student will learn about daily living skills.	Have students do a one day observation of all the activities undertaken in their homes to live on a day-to-day basis. Students' lists should include things like grocery shopping, cooking, housekeeping, and making phone calls for services. Then use the list and incorporate relevant lessons into student's class work.
33. The student will have appropriate manners and personal habits.	Enlist the help of business owners in your area. Have them speak to students about expectations for employee behavior with customers, supervisors, and co-workers. Have them also address personal hygiene, habits, and dress. Arrange for individual instruction for students needing more guidance with their manners and habits by a staff member, like the school social worker or the work experience coordinator.

Individual Objective	Strategy or Intervention
34. The student will handle gossip and rumors appropriately.	If a student finds himself the victim of gossip or rumors, encourage him to come to you or another staff member to discuss the situation before reacting and worsening the situation. Have the student anticipate the consequences of various ways of handling the situation before actually taking action.
35. The student will avoid blaming others.	Blaming others often occurs as a "face-saving" tactic when a student is confronted publicly. Whenever a need occurs to confront a student about a problem or situation, meet with the student privately outside of class. Use the time to share perspectives and problem solve together. Encourage the student to use a similar approach when facing a situation elsewhere. He can ask the involved individual to discuss the situation at a better time when they can talk privately without interruption.
36. The student will be able to handle unexpected situations and emergencies.	Prepare a card for the student with common emergency phone numbers. Make a copy so the student can put one card near his phone and carry a copy with him. Pose typical emergency situations for the student and have him tell how he'd handle them. Situations might include missing a ride or the bus, getting ill at school, or handling a work conflict.

Parent's Name and Work Number: _____
Relative's Name and Work Number: _____
Your Work Phone Number: _____
Doctor's Name and Phone Number: _____
Dentist's Name and Phone Number: _____

Appendices

Behavior Improvement Form

Student _____   Observer _____

Situation or Class _____   Date _____

    A. Brief Description of Problem Behavior

    B. Concrete Explanation and Examples of Behavior

    C. What do you think the student is escaping, avoiding, or "getting" through this behavior?

    D. Are there any particular settings, environments, or circumstances that may be causing or affecting this behavior?

    E. What behavior does the student need to learn instead (the replacement behavior)? And/or what changes may need to be made in the student's environment?

    F. With the student, write down ways to learn and practice the replacement behavior.

Sample Behavior Improvement Form

Student ___Adam_____   Observer ___Ms. Juarez_____

Situation or Class ___Language Arts_____   Date ___Nov. 8_____

A. Brief Description of Problem Behavior

Adam is extremely disruptive during independent seat work time.

B. Concrete Explanation and Examples of Behavior

Adam interrupts other students who are working. He also has to frequently get up to sharpen and "resharpen" his pencil.

C. What do you think the student is escaping, avoiding, or "getting" through this behavior?

Adam could be avoiding doing the work because it's too difficult.

Maybe Adam has trouble physically with writing and doing written work.

Adam may not understand the directions and not know how to ask for clarification.

D. Are there any particular settings, environments, or circumstances that may be causing or affecting this behavior?

Adam is more distractible when he has to work on his own. He may benefit from working in an area that is less visually or auditorially distracting, like in a study carrel or at a more isolated computer station.

E. What behavior does the student need to learn instead (the replacement behavior)? And/or what changes may need to be made in the student's environment?

Adam needs to let the teacher know what he needs to be able to do the seat work, like the following:
- directions explained more
- use of computer instead of handwriting
- shorter assignment

F. With the student, write down ways to learn and practice the replacement behavior.

Adam will check his understanding of assignment directions with the teacher before he begins work.

Adam will ask to be allowed to use the computer in the back of the room to word process his longer assignments

Behavior Assessment Form

Student _____   Date _____

Class/Setting _____   Teacher/Staff Member _____

1. What specific behavior is an issue in your classroom or setting? Describe how the behavior is a problem.

2. Under which circumstances does the behavior occur? For example, does the student act this way with certain individuals, outside or inside the classroom, or during unstructured times?

3. Based on your observation, what happens before the behavior occurs?

4. How have teachers, administrators, peers, and parents reacted to the student's behavior?

5. What happens to the student's behavior when teachers, administrators, peers, or parents react to it? Does it change in any way?

6. Why do you think the student behaves in this manner? What does he or she hope to gain by it?

7. What strengths and competencies does the student have?

8. Does the student seem to understand the consequences of his or her behavior? How do you know?

Behavior Tracking Sheet

Student _____

Observer _____ Title _____

Behavior to Observe _____

_____

Student   is / is not   aware of the observation. (Circle one.)

Date	Class/Situation	Number of Times Observed

Sample Behavior Tracking Sheet

Student   _Cody L._

Observer   _Jim Sullivan_   Title   _School Psychologist_

Behavior to Observe   _Cody frequently uses profanity and also makes suggestive,_

inappropriate comments.

Student   is / (is not)   aware of the observation.   (Circle one.)

Date	Class/Situation	Number of Times Observed
9/15	English class in BD room	Profanity ### /// Suggestive Comments //
9/18	Regular Science class	Profanity //// Suggestive Comments /
9/22	Library trip	Profanity /// Suggestive Comments 0

Appendices
The Behavior Disorder IEP Companion   144   Copyright © 2003 LinguiSystems, Inc.
Appendices
The Behavior Disorder IEP Companion   144   Copyright © 2003 LinguiSystems, Inc.

Student Behavior Survey

Your Name _____   Date _____

Grade _____

1. What behavior is getting you in trouble at school?

   _____

   _____

2. Describe when you do this or act this way. Where are you, when is it happening, and who are you with?

   _____

   _____

3. Why do you think you are acting like this?

   _____

   _____

4. What have the school, your teachers, or parents done to help you?

   _____

   _____

5. What will happen if you keep acting this way or have this problem?

   _____

   _____

6. What do you think needs to happen to get you to improve this behavior?

   _____

   _____

Work Completion Sheet

Student _____   Date _____

Class _____   Assignment or Task _____

       ❑ Check 1

       ❑ Check 2

       ❑ Check 3

       ❑ Check 4

       ❑ Completed

Work Completion Sheet

Student _____   Date _____

Class _____   Assignment or Task _____

       ❑ Check 1

       ❑ Check 2

       ❑ Check 3

       ❑ Check 4

       ❑ Completed

Assignment Sheet

Class	Assignment	Teacher Initials	Parent Initials

Lesson Activities Sheet

Lesson _____

Whole class: _____
_____
_____
_____

Individual Choices: Choose one of these follow-up activities.

1. _____
_____
_____
_____

2. _____
_____
_____
_____

3. _____
_____
_____
_____

4. _____
_____
_____
_____

Story Mapping Worksheet

1. Write the story title on the line.

2. Write what you think the story will be about on the line.

3. Read half the story.

4. Fill in the story map with the name and description of important characters you know so far.

5. Finish reading the story.

6. Fill in the most important events that happened, including the story's ending.

7. Add any other characters and descriptions to the story map.

Story Title _____

I think the story will be about _____.

Character Name

Character Description

Character Name

Character Description

Character Name

Character Description

Character Name

Character Description

Event

Event

Event

Event

Request for Accommodations

Class:

Assignment:

Skills Needed:

Time Given:

Accommodations: _____ will need:
                          student

1. _____

   _____

2. _____

   _____

3. _____

   _____

Date: **Teacher**:

Group Planning Sheet

Assignment:

Group:

Role of Group Member 1:

Responsibility:

Role of Group Member 2:

Responsibility:

Role of Group Member 3:

Responsibility:

Role of Group Member 4:

Responsibility:

Class Sign-In Sheet

Class _____

Period _____

Teacher _____

Student's Name	Time In	Minutes Late/ On Time	Reason

Observation Sheet

Student Name _____

Observer _____

Date	Class	Behaviors Observed	Number of Times Observed

Voice Volume Indicator

Copy the dial and pointer on sturdier paper. Attach the pointer to the dial with a fastener. Move the pointer to show the volume you want students to use for each situation.

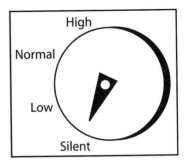

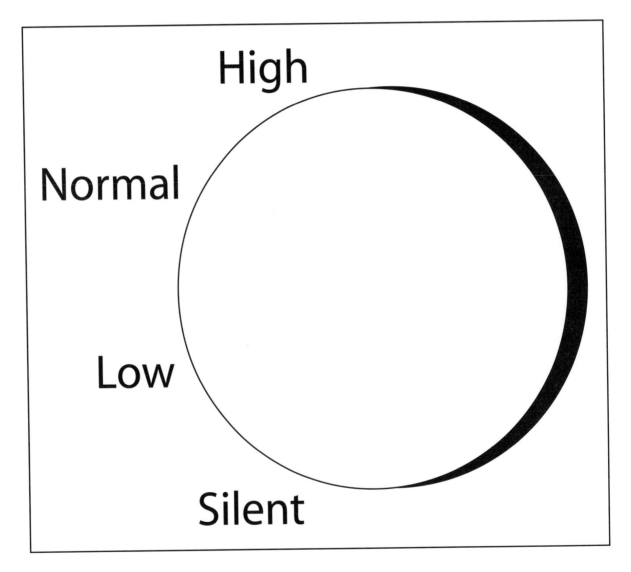

Classroom Rules of Respect

1. **Respect the adult in charge.**
   Look, listen, and cooperate.

2. **Respect each other.**
   Use "please" and "thank you."

3. **Respect your classroom.**
   Take care of the room and materials in it.

Coping with Conflict (Student-Teacher)

Situation:

Student Reaction: _____

_____

_____

_____

Teacher Reaction: _____

_____

_____

_____

Better Student
Reaction: _____

_____

_____

_____

Teacher Reaction: _____

_____

_____

_____

Coping with Conflict (Student-Peer)

Situation:

Student Reaction: _____

_____

_____

_____

Peer Reactions: _____

_____

_____

_____

Better Student
Reaction: _____

_____

_____

_____

Peer Reactions: _____

_____

_____

_____

Problem-Solving Tips

Use these steps to handle conflicts positively and productively.

 Pose the problem. State the conflict in just a few words.

 Scan through your choices. Think of at least three ways the conflict might be handled.

 Take action. Think through the possible effects of each choice. Take action with the choice that best solves the conflict.

Discussion Guidelines

1. Raise your hand.

2. Wait patiently for the teacher to call on you.

3. Give your ideas or answer.

4. Say, "I'm done" to show that someone else can now talk.

Effects of Positive and Negative Behaviors

Positive Behavior	Effect

Negative Behavior	Effect

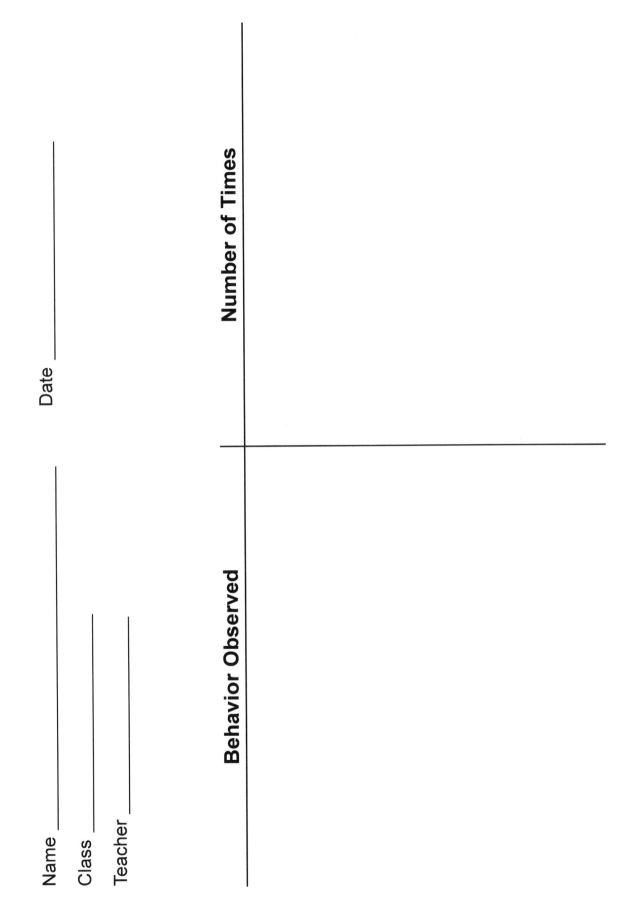

Behavior Observation Chart

Name _____

Class _____

Teacher _____

Date _____

Number of Times

Behavior Observed

Situation Picture

_____

Caption

Turn-Taking Record Sheet

Group _____

Week _____

Activity _____

Dates

Order of Turns						
First						
Second						
Third						
Fourth						
Fifth						

_____'s Materials Sign-Out Sheet

Be sure to sign this sheet when you take things from my "warehouse"!

Student's Name	Date	Item Borrowed	Condition When Returned

Feeling Rater

How would you rate this situation? Are you happy, sad, hurt, disappointed, or angry?

Name your feeling. _____ Then rate it on the Feeling Rater.

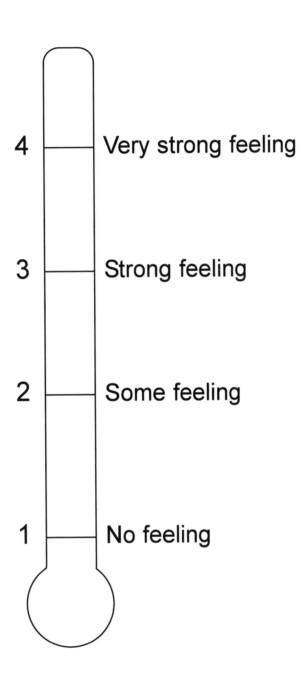

4   Very strong feeling

3   Strong feeling

2   Some feeling

1   No feeling

Daily Feeling Journal

Date _____

How are you feeling today?

What is making you feel this way?

How are your feelings affecting how your day is going?

What are you feeling particularly good about? Why?

Handle Conflicts Positively

Conflicts don't just disappear. You need to handle them positively in order to make the best of the situation. Fill in the steps below to help you through the conflict resolution process.

1. What is the conflict or problem?

2. Who or what do you have a conflict with? Why?

3. What do you want to happen instead?

4. What can you say or do to request what you want?

5. In what way should you say or do it?

6. Where should you say or do it?

Planning a Win-Win Compromise

Situation:

Name who might win or lose in each section below. Then describe the possible outcomes.

Win-Lose: _____ wins.

_____ loses.

_____

_____

_____

Lose-Win: _____ wins.

_____ loses.

_____

_____

_____

Win-Win: _____ and

_____ both win.

_____

_____

_____

Thinking Through a Decision

My Decision

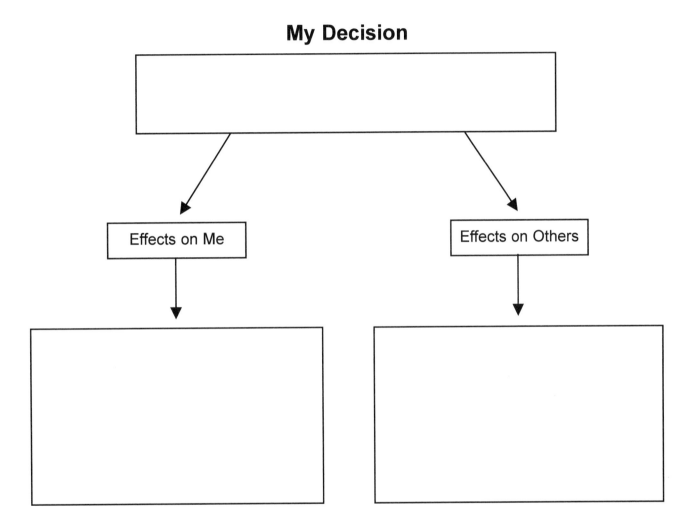

Effects on Me

Effects on Others

Record of Inappropriate Comments

Name _____

Date _____

Situation or Class _____

Teacher _____

Frequency	When	What Kind of Comment	To Whom

Stop to Think

1. What will I say?

2. What will I do?

3. What might happen because of what I do or say?

4. Should I do it? Why?

Problem-Solving Journal

Problem-solving situation:

Rating:

Solution:

Problem-solving situation:

Rating:

Solution:

Problem-solving situation:

Rating:

Solution:

What's Your Mood?

Fill in the following statements.

1. I'm in a _____ mood.

2. I feel this way because _____
   _____
   _____
   _____
   _____

3. My mood might affect other people by _____
   _____
   _____
   _____
   _____

4. My mood will go away or get better once _____
   _____
   _____
   _____
   _____

Self-Defeating Behaviors

Behavior	Reaction of Others	Better Choice
Whining	Irritated by you Make fun of you Avoid you and don't help	Try it before making any comment. Ask for help. Make a suggestion in a nice way.
Being Negative	Think you have a bad attitude Leave you out because you're hard to get along with	Give something a chance. Say something positively.
Procrastinating	Think you're lazy Think you don't care Think you can't do it Think you're undependable	Ask for help. Ask for more time. Suggest a different way. Tell what you've done and when you'll be finished.
Avoidance	Think you can't do it Think you're not responsible Think you can't be trusted	Ask for help. Work it out with the person. Be honest.

Goal-Setting Form

Goal _____   Today's Date _____

Materials/Resources _____

_____

_____

Time Needed _____   Due Date _____

How Success Will Be Measured _____

_____

_____

Goal-Setting Form

Goal _____   Today's Date _____

Materials/Resources _____

_____

_____

Time Needed _____   Due Date _____

How Success Will Be Measured _____

_____

_____

Academic Plans

Freshman Year Academic Plan		
Required Classes	Classes for Career Exploration	Classes to Meet Individual Needs

Sophomore Year Academic Plan		
Required Classes	Classes for Career Exploration	Classes to Meet Individual Needs

Academic Plans, continued

Junior Year Academic Plan		
Required Classes	Classes for Career Exploration	Classes to Meet Individual Needs

Senior Year Academic Plan		
Required Classes	Classes for Career Exploration	Classes to Meet Individual Needs

References

American Psychiatric Association. (1994). *Diagnostic and statistical manual of mental disorders (DSM-IV)* (4th ed.). Washington, DC: Author.

Armstrong, Thomas. (1995). *The myth of the A.D.D. child—50 ways to improve your child's behavior and attention span without drugs, labels, or coercion.* NY: The Penguin Group.

Bowman, Robert P., Carr, Tom, Cooper, Kathy, Miles, Ron, & Toner, Tommie. (1998). *Innovative strategies for unlocking difficult adolescents.* Chapin, SC: Youth Light, Inc.

Brown, Molly Lyle. (2002). *The ADHD Companion.* East Moline, IL: LinguiSystems, Inc.

Burke, Kay. (1992). *What to do with the kid who . . . , Developing cooperation, self-discipline, and responsibility in the classroom K-12.* Palatine, IL: Skylight Publishing.

Campbell, Pam, & Siperstein, Gary N. (1994). *Improving social competence—A resource for elementary school teachers.* Boston: Allyn and Bacon.

Canter, Lee, & Canter, Marlene. (1993). *Succeeding with difficult students: New strategies for reaching your most challenging students.* Santa Monica, CA: Lee Canter & Associates.

Center for Effective Collaboration and Practice. *Addressing student problem behavior.* http://cecp.air.org/fba/problembehavior/text.htm#Behavior%201Intervention%20Plans

Levin, James, & Shanken-Kaye, John M. (1996). *The self-control classroom: Understanding and managing the disruptive behavior of all students, including those with ADHD.* Dubuque, IA: Kendall/Hunt Publishing Company.

Levine, Mel. Behavioral complications (video and guide booklet) from *Developing minds video library.* (2002). Boston: WGBH Educational Foundation in association with All Kinds of Minds. *www.allkindsofminds.org   www.wgbh.org*

McGinnis, Ellen, & Goldstein, Arnold P. (1997). *Skillstreaming the elementary school child: New strategies and perspectives for teaching prosocial skills.* Champaign, IL: Research Press.

Mississippi Bend Area Education Agency. (2002, May). *Special education entitlement criteria, K-12.* Bettendorf, IA: Author.

Rosenberg, Michael S., Wilson, Rich, Maheady, Larry, & Sindelar, Paul T. (1992). *Educating students with behavior disorders.* Boston: Allyn and Bacon.

Shapiro, Edward S., & Cole, Christine L. (1994). *Behavior change in the classroom—Self-management interventions.* NY: The Guilford Press.

The ERIC Clearinghouse on Disabilities and Gifted Education. (1999). Positive behavior support and functional assessment. *http://ericec.org/digests/e580.html*

U.S. National Archives and Records Administration. Emotional behavior disorders. (1999, March 12). *Federal Register.* Washington, DC: Author.

Vernon, Ann. (1989). *Thinking, feeling, behaving: An emotional education curriculum for children—Grades 1-6.* Champaign, IL: Research Press.

Vernon, Ann. (1989). *Thinking, feeling, behaving: An emotional education curriculum for adolescents—Grades 7-12.* Champaign, IL: Research Press.

21-04-98765432